Markus Kristan

export

Austrian Architecture in Europe

Österreichische Architekten bauen für Europa

SpringerWienNewYork

.KUNST
bundeskanzleramt

Printed in Austria

Gedruckt mit Unterstützung von
Bundeskanzleramt — Sektion Kunst

Coverfoto | Coverphoto:
© Vulcania—Joël Damase, Europäisches Zentrum für Vulkanismus, Clermont-Ferrand, 1994–2002, Kegelinneres, Architect: Hans Hollein

Frontispiz | Frontispiece:
© Gustav Peichl Kunst und Ausstellungshalle der Bundesrepublik Deutschland, Bonn, 1986–1992, Lichttürme, Architect: Gustav Peichl

Einbandrückseite | Backcover:
© Gerald Zugmann, UFA Kino Palast, Dresden, 1993-1998, Außenansicht, Architect: Coop Himmelb(l)au

Herausgeber und Autor | Editor and Author: Markus Kristan
Übersetzung | Translation: Pedro M. López
Konzept und Gestaltung | Concept and design:
Markus Kristan | David Marold, Springer-Verlag
Druck | Printing:
A. Holzhausens Nfg., A-1140 Wien
Repro | Reproduction p 39–43: Pixelstorm, A-1190 Wien

Gedruckt auf säurefreiem, chlorfrei gebleichtem Papier – TCF
Printed on acid-free and chlorine-free bleached paper

SPIN: 10885428

Bibliographische Information Der Deutschen Bibliothek
Die Deutsche Bibliothek verzeichnet diese Publikation in der Deutschen Nationalbibliographie; detaillierte bibliographische Daten sind im Internet über <http://dnb.ddb.de> abrufbar.

Mit zahlreichen Abbildungen
With numerous Figures

ISBN 3-211-83842-2 Springer-Verlag Wien New York

Preface | Vorwort

Building in Europe! An Austrian architect's dream! Many paths lead to this goal and Austrian architects have followed them throughout the past decades - from participating in international competitions to collaborating with foreign construction authorities and opening their own offices across Europe.

Otto Wagner and his immediate successors were generally unsuccessful with their competition entries. Although their proposals often won awards, they were rarely realized. It was only at the end of the 20th century that Austrian architects such as Gustav Peichl, Wilhelm Holzbauer, Hans Hollein and Coop Himmelb(l)au were commissioned to complete important construction projects abroad.

During the economically difficult years in Austria between the two wars, many architects were forced to leave the country. Anton Brenner, Margarete Lihotzky and Franz Schuster were given the chance of working for the construction authorities in Frankfurt/Main, Germany, while Roland Rainer was given work at the Academy for Urban Construction in Berlin.

Austrian architects have opened offices beyond their borders for around 100 years, e.g. Joseph Maria Olbrich in Darmstadt and Düsseldorf, Josef Frank in Stockholm, Michael Rosenauer in London, Wilhelm Holzbauer in Amsterdam, Ortner & Ortner in Berlin and Dietmar Feichtinger

Bauen in Europa! Ein österreichischer Architektentraum! Die Wege zur Erreichung dieses Zieles sind vielfältig, und sie wurden alle von österreichischen Architekten in den vergangenen Jahrzehnten beschritten - von der Beteiligung an internationalen Wettbewerben über direkte Aufträge aus dem Ausland bis zur Mitarbeit in ausländischen Bauämtern und Eröffnung eigener Ateliers in Europa.

Otto Wagner und seine unmittelbaren Nachfolger waren mit ihren Wettbewerbsbeiträgen zumeist nicht erfolgreich. Ihre Konkurrenzprojekte wurden zwar oft prämiert aber kaum je realisiert. Erst gegen Ende des 20. Jahrhunderts errangen österreichische Architekten wie Gustav Peichl, Wilhelm Holzbauer, Hans Hollein und Coop Himmelb(l)au Aufträge für wichtige Bauten.

In der in Österreich wirtschaftlich schwierigen Zwischenkriegszeit waren viele Architekten gezwungen, das Land zu verlassen. Anton Brenner, Margarete Lihotzky und Franz Schuster etwa hatten Gelegenheit für das Bauamt in Frankfurt/Main zu arbeiten. Roland Rainer war an der Städtebau-Akademie in Berlin tätig.

Seit rund 100 Jahren eröffneten österreichische Architekten außerhalb der Grenzen ihrer Heimat Ateliers. Z. B.: Joseph Maria Olbrich in Darmstadt und Düsseldorf, Josef Frank in Stockholm, Michael Rosenauer in London, Wilhelm Holzbauer in Amsterdam, Ortner & Ortner in Berlin und

in Paris. In these cases, Austria not only exported its architecture, but also its architects as well.

Architecture as an exportable product! A fascinating thought! Austrian architectural thought that has become a reality can be admired in almost all European countries, and projects were completed in all fields: churches, city halls, universities, operas, theaters, museums, exhibition pavilions, factories, office buildings, residential projects and housing, as well as villas and bridges.

This publication is divided into three sections. The first section discusses buildings and projects that were completed between 1900 and 1980. The second section, which constitutes the main focus of the book, concentrates on the most important projects completed by Austrian architects outside of Austria's borders on European soil between 1980 and 2002. The third section of this publication presents projects that are currently under construction and others which will be completed in the near future. An addendum contains short biographies of the architects whose projects were completed between 1980 and 2002.

Dietmar Feichtinger in Paris. In diesen Fällen exportierte Österreich nicht nur seine Architektur, sondern seine Architekten gleich noch mit dazu.

Architektur als Exportartikel! Ein Gedanke, der fasziniert! Gebaute Ideen von österreichischen Architekten gibt es in nahezu allen Ländern Europas, wobei Bauten für sämtliche Bauaufgaben verwirklicht wurden: Kirchen, Rathäuser, Universitäten, Opern, Theater, Museen, Ausstellungspavillons, Fabriken, Bürohäuser, Wohnhäuser, Villen und Brücken.

Die vorliegende Publikation ist in drei Abschnitte unterteilt. Der erste Abschnitt behandelt Bauten und Projekte, die im Zeitraum zwischen 1900 und 1980 entstanden. Im zweiten Abschnitt, der den Schwerpunkt des Buches bildet, werden einige der bedeutendsten, zwischen 1980 und 2002 errichteten Leistungen österreichischer Architekten außerhalb der Grenzen Österreichs auf europäischem Boden vorgeführt. Der dritte Abschnitt dieser Veröffentlichung stellt einige Projekte vor, die gerade gebaut werden oder in naher Zukunft realisiert werden sollen. In einem Anhang sind Kurzbiographien der Architekten aufgenommen, deren zwischen 1980 und 2002 errichtete Bauten dargestellt wurden.

Table of Contents | Inhalt

export 1900—1980

Otto Wagner, German Reichstag Building, Berlin, 1882

Modern Austrian architecture began with OTTO WAGNER **(1841 Vienna-Penzing – 1918 Vienna). Things began in September 1894 or, to be precise, when** OTTO WAGNER **was chosen to succeed** CARL VON HASENAUER**, who passed away at the beginning of 1894, as the Director of the Special Architecture School at the Academy of Fine Arts in Vienna. Until then,** WAGNER **had constructed Renaissance style buildings and had already made a name for himself as an architecture theoretician. The selection committee therefore considered him an ideal successor to** HASENAUER**, who also preferred the Renaissance style for his buildings. The shock must have been immense when the hitherto conservative** OTTO WAGNER**, who was already past middle age, suddenly developed into an almost avantgarde architect within a few months. This transformation is always explained as having been the result of the influence of his collaborators and pupils.** MAX FABIANI, JOSEPH MARIA OLBRICH, JOSEF HOFFMANN **and Josef Plečnik deserve particular mention in this context. Projects and buildings that delineated the path of Austrian architecture into the 20th century were conceived in a concentrated atmosphere, in which the aging master and his circle inspired one another. Once this course was taken, it was accelerated and reinforced by the establishment of the Vienna Secession in 1897 and the establishment of the Wiener Werkstätte Studios in 1903.**

Aside from the Synagogue completed in Budapest in 1868, which was part of the Austro-Hungarian empire as the Capital

Moderne Architektur beginnt in Österreich mit OTTO WAGNER (1841 Wien-Penzing – 1918 Wien). Sie beginnt genau im September 1894. In diesem Monat trat OTTO WAGNER die Nachfolge des Anfang 1894 verstorbenen CARL VON HASENAUER als Leiter einer Spezialschule für Architektur an der Akademie der bildenden Künste in Wien an. WAGNER hatte bis dahin im Stil der Renaissance gebaut und sich bereits als Architekturtheoretiker einen Namen gemacht. Die Berufungskommission glaubte daher in ihm den idealen Nachfolger des gleichfalls im Renaissancestil bauenden CARL VON HASENAUER gefunden zu haben. Wie groß muss die Überraschung, um nicht zu sagen der Schock, gewesen sein, als sich gleichsam innerhalb weniger Monate aus dem konservativen, bereits die Lebensmitte überschritten habenden OTTO WAGNER ein nahezu avantgardistischer Architekt entwickelte. Diese Wandlung wird immer mit dem Einfluss seiner jungen Mitarbeiter und Schüler erklärt. Für diese erste Zeit sind besonders MAX FABIANI, JOSEPH MARIA OLBRICH, JOSEF HOFFMANN und Josef Plečnik zu nennen. In einer konzentrierten Atmosphäre, in der sich der ältere Meister und sein Kreis gegenseitig inspirierten, entstanden Projekte und Bauten, die den Weg für die Architektur des 20. Jahrhunderts in Österreich ebneten. Dieser einmal eingeschlagene Weg wurde durch die Gründung der Wiener Secession 1897 und durch die Gründung der Wiener Werkstätte 1903 noch beschleunigt und verstärkt.

Abgesehen von der 1868 ausgeführten Synagoge in Budapest, das damals als

Otto Wagner, High Altitude Sunlight Spa, Palmschos / Brixen, Southern Tyrol, 1913/14

of Hungary, OTTO WAGNER **was not able to build any of his many – often award-winning – projects for European competitions. Most of the known competition projects stem from the time before 1894, when he accepted his chair as professor at the Academy of Fine Arts in Vienna.**

In 1867, when he was only 26, WAGNER **submitted an entry for the Berlin Dome project. Wagner's next international project, the design of the Lemberg (Lvov) Regional Parliament Building in 1875 project was purchased. A series of competition projects followed afterwards: The Hamburg City Hall (1876), the Soborsin (Romania) Parish Church (1879), the German Reichstag Building in Berlin (1882), the Budapest Parliament (1882/83), the Amsterdam Stock Exchange (1884), the second Berlin Dome Project (1890/91) and the Catholic Parish Church in Esseg/Slavonia (Croatia) in (1893). After an interval, when he was already professor of the special architecture class at the Academy of Fine Arts in Vienna, he submitted competition entries for the Patras/Greece Cathedral (1902) and the Palace of Peace in The Hague/Holland (1905). In 1913/14, on the eve of WWI,** WAGNER **designed a project for the high altitude sunlight spa in Palmschos close to Brixen in Southern Tyrol, Italy, which was also never built.**

The generation that followed OTTO WAGNER **had more success abroad. Some of these were members of the socalled "Wagner Circle," which consisted of** MAX FABIANI, JOSEPH MARIA OLBRICH **and** JOSEF HOFFMANN, **as well as the exceptional** ADOLF LOOS, **who was**

Hauptstadt von Ungarn Teil der Doppelmonarchie war, konnte OTTO WAGNER keines seiner zahlreichen - zumeist prämierten - Wettbewerbsprojekte für das europäische Ausland verwirklichen. Die meisten der bekannten Konkurrenzprojekte stammen aus der Zeit vor 1894, noch bevor er seine Professur an der Akademie der bildenden Künste in Wien erhielt.

Bereits als 26jähriger nahm er 1867 am Wettbewerb für den Dom in Berlin teil. WAGNERS nächstes internationales Wettbewerbsprojekt von 1875 für das Landtagsgebäude in Lemberg wurde durch Ankauf ausgezeichnet. Es folgten in dichter zeitlicher Reihenfolge die Wettbewerbsprojekte für das Rathaus in Hamburg (1876), für die Pfarrkirche in Soborsin (Rumänien) (1879), für das Deutsche Reichstagsgebäude in Berlin (1882), das Parlamentsgebäude in Budapest (1882/83), das Börsengebäude in Amsterdam (1884), das zweite Projekt für den Dom in Berlin (1890/91) und die katholische Pfarrkirche in Esseg/Slavonien (1893). Mit einigem zeitlichen Abstand, schon in seiner Zeit als Leiter der Spezialklasse für Architektur an der Akademie der bildenden Künste in Wien, entstanden die Wettbewerbsprojekte für die Kathedrale in Patras/Griechenland (1902) und den Friedenspalast in Den Haag (1905). Gleichsam am Vorabend des Ersten Weltkrieges, 1913/14, schuf WAGNER ein Projekt für eine Höhen- und Sonnenlicht-Heilstätte in Palmschos bei Brixen/Südtirol, die ebenfalls nicht ausgeführt wurde.

Wesentlich erfolgreicher außerhalb der Grenzen Österreichs als OTTO WAGNER

Max Fabiani, Girls' School, Ljubljana, 1897–1901

Max Fabiani, Casa Bartoli, Trieste, 1905–08

a loner initially. These architects, who were born between 1865 and 1870, were not only given the opportunity of planning in Europe, but also of building their projects. This could have been a sign of how times had changed since WAGNER'S **day, but it was also evidence of travels and longer stays abroad on the part of Austrian architects. All in all, Austrian architecture seems to have been better able to compete abroad during this period.**

The oldest of the architects listed above was MAX FABIANI **(1865 Kobdil/Slovenia – 1962 Görz). Despite his family's Italian descent he was raised as an Austrian and grew up speaking three languages (German, Italian, Slovenian). After winning the Ghega Prize he set off on a tour of Europe that took him to England, Belgium, France, Germany, Greece and Italy.**

Due to his trilingual upbringing, Fabiani's planning and construction activities abroad were extensive. The title of his biography "Ein Architekt der Monarchie" (An Architect of the Monarchy) by Marco Pozzetto is therefore more appropriate for him than for any other one of his colleagues. He created urban planning proposals for Ljubljana, Slovenia, Bielsko-Biala in Poland and Görz. Some of his public buildings and residential projects were built, primarily in Görz, Llubljana and Trieste.

The following examples should be listed here: his urban planning concept for Ljubljana (1895–1960), his health resort for Imperial state officials in Abbazia (today's Opatija) (1897), the residential and commercial project for the Trieste Savings and Loan Bank and

war die auf ihm nachfolgende Generation. Der sogenannte Wagnerkreis mit MAX FABIANI, JOSEPH MARIA OLBRICH und JOSEF HOFFMANN sowie als Ausnahmeerscheinung und vorerst Einzelgänger ADOLF LOOS. Diese zwischen 1865 und 1870 geborenen Architekten sowie andere hatten wiederholt Gelegenheit nicht nur für Europa zu planen sondern auch zu bauen. Dies mag an der gegenüber WAGNER veränderten Zeit gelegen sein, in der sie tätig waren, aber zum Teil auch an der großen Reisetätigkeit und den längeren Auslandsaufenthalten. Insgesamt scheint österreichische Architektur in dieser Periode im Ausland konkurrenzfähiger geworden zu sein.

Der älteste der oben genannten Architekten ist MAX FABIANI (1865 Kobdil/Slowenien – 1962 Görz). Trotz der italienischen Herkunft seiner Familie erhielt er eine österreichische Erziehung und wuchs dreisprachig (deutsch, italienisch, slowenisch) auf. Als Träger des Ghega-Preises trat er 1892 eine Europareise an, die ihn nach England, Belgien, Frankreich, Deutschland, Griechenland und Italien führte.

Bedingt durch seine dreisprachige Erziehung ist seine Planungs- und Bautätigkeit außerhalb der Grenzen des heutigen Österreichs reichhaltig und der Titel seiner Biographie „Ein Architekt der Monarchie" von Marco Pozzetto trifft auf ihn wohl besser als auf irgend einen anderen seiner Berufskollegen zu. Er schuf städtebauliche Planungen für Laibach, Bielsko-Biala in Polen und Görz. Öffentliche Bauten und Wohnbauten entstanden vor allem in Görz, Laibach und Triest.

Joseph Maria Olbrich, Wedding Tower and Exhibition Building, Darmstadt, 1905–08

Joseph Maria Olbrich, Tietz Department Store, Düsseldorf, 1906–08

the Slovenian Community Center in Trieste (1902).

JOSEPH MARIA OLBRICH **(1867 Troppau/Silesia–1908 Düsseldorf) completed his studies under** OTTO WAGNER'S **predecessor, Carl von Hasenauer. In 1893, he received the "Prix de Rome" and traveled to Italy and North Africa. In 1898,** OLBRICH **designed the "Café Niedermeyer" in his hometown of Troppau, but it was never built. He created a 'Wiener Interieur' (Viennese Interior) for the World Fair held in Paris in 1900. He was invited to join the artistic community in Darmstadt by Grand Duke Ernst Ludwig and moved to Hesse in 1899. In Hesse, he supervised construction at the Darmstadt Mathildenhöhe (Mathilda Heights) for eight years. Seven buildings were built by 1901, one of them his own house as well as the small and large Glückert Houses and the building for mural art. He created a number of exhibition facilities on Mathildenhöhe, such as those for the 1901 exhibition "Ein Dokument deutscher Kunst" (A Document of German Art), as well as the Ernst-Ludwig-Haus. In 1908, he completed the "Hochzeitsturm" (Wedding Tower) a permanent building as a gift to the city of Darmstadt from Grand Duke Ernst Ludwig. The building was connected to a large-surface exhibition building. In the same year,** OLBRICH **moved to Düsseldorf, although he kept his studio in Darmstadt. He built a number of single-family houses in Cologne. These villas, Clarenbach House in Witlaer near Düsseldorf, and the Tietz department store building in Düsseldorf, which he had begun building in 1906, marked his**

Beispielhaft seien hier genannt: die städtebauliche Planung für Laibach (1895–1960), Kurhaus für k. u. k. Staatsbeamte in Abbazia (heute Opatija) (1897), Wohn- und Geschäftshaus der Sparkasse Triest und slowenisches Gemeinschaftszentrum in Triest (1902).

JOSEPH MARIA OLBRICH (1867 Troppau/Schlesien – 1908 Düsseldorf) schloss sein Studium bei OTTO WAGNERS Vorgänger an der Akademie der bildenden Künste, bei CARL VON HASENAUER, ab. 1893 erhielt er den „Prix de Rome" und reiste nach Italien und Nordafrika. 1898 plante OLBRICH für seine Heimatstadt Troppau das „Café Niedermeyer", das jedoch nicht realisiert wurde. Mit einem „Wiener Interieur" nahm er 1900 an der Weltausstellung in Paris teil. Aufgrund seiner Berufung an die Darmstädter Künstlerkolonie durch den Großherzog Ernst Ludwig übersiedelte er 1899 nach Hessen und hatte auf der Darmstädter Mathildenhöhe acht Jahre lang die Bauleitung inne. Bis 1901 entstanden sieben Häuser, darunter auch sein eigenes, das kleine und das große Haus Glückert sowie das Gebäude für Flächenkunst. 1901 schuf er auch für die Ausstellung „Ein Dokument deutscher Kunst" zahlreiche Ausstellungsbauten auf der Mathildenhöhe, wie das Ernst-Ludwig-Haus. Als bleibendes Bauwerk wurde 1908 der „Hochzeitsturm" als Geschenk der Stadt Darmstadt an den Großherzog Ernst Ludwig fertiggestellt, dem ein weitläufiges Ausstellungsgebäude angeschlossen war. Unter Beibehaltung seines Darmstädter Ateliers zog OLBRICH im selben Jahr nach Düsseldorf. Von dort aus errichtete er in Köln einige

Josef Hoffmann, Austrian Pavilion for the 1934 Venice Biennial Exhibition

Josef Hoffmann, Palais Stoclet, Brussels, 1906–11

transition to a monumental neo-Classicist style.

JOSEF HOFFMANN'S **(1870 Pirnitz/Southern Moravia – 1956 Vienna) most famous building outside of Austria is the Palais Stoclet in Brussels. The Belgian patrons of the arts, Adolphe and Suzanne Stoclet lived in Vienna between 1904/5 and became acquainted with** HOFFMANN'S **villas in the Hohe Warte area of Vienna's 19th district, which made a lasting impression on them. When Adolphe Stoclet's father passed away, he was forced to return to Brussels. In 1906, he commissioned** HOFFMANN **to complete what is probably the most valuable, complete Jugendstil work of art that exists.**

HOFFMANN **built a number of pavilions for large international exhibitions throughout Europe before WWI and between the two wars. In 1911, he created the Austrian pavilion for the International Art Fair in Rome. The German Werkbund exhibition opened in Cologne on 16 May 1914, right before the outbreak of WWI.** HOFFMANN **was in charge of building the Austria House for this exhibition. In France between 1924 and 1925,** HOFFMANN **collaborated with** OSWALD HAERDTL **and Max Fellerer, on the Austrian pavilion for the 1925 Exposition Internationale des Arts Décoratifs et Industriels Modernes (Paris International Decorative Arts and Crafts Fair). Individual construction segments of the overall concept devised by** HOFFMANN **were contributed by Peter Behrens,** JOSEF FRANK **and Oskar Strnad. The last high point of** HOFFMANN'S **pavilion work was the Austrian Pavilion for the 1934**

Einfamilienhäuser. Mit diesen Villen sowie dem Haus Clarenbach in Wittlaer bei Düsseldorf und dem bereits 1906 begonnenen Warenhaus Tietz für Düsseldorf wechselte er zu einem monumentalen Neoklassizismus.

JOSEF HOFFMANNS (1870 Pirnitz/Südmähren – 1956 Wien) bekanntester Bau außerhalb der Grenzen Österreichs ist das Palais Stoclet in Brüssel. 1904/05 wohnten die belgischen Kunstmäzene Adolphe und Suzanne Stoclet in Wien und lernten hier die Villenbauten HOFFMANNS auf der Hohen Warte kennen, die sie tief beeindruckten. Als Adolphe Stoclets Vater starb, musste er nach Brüssel zurückkehren. 1906 erteilte er HOFFMANN den Auftrag für das wohl wertvollste Gesamtkunstwerk des Jugendstils.

Vor dem Ersten Weltkrieg und auch in der Zwischenkriegszeit errichtete HOFFMANN zahlreiche Pavillons bei den großen internationalen Ausstellungen in Europa. 1911 schuf er den Österreichischen Pavillon auf der Internationalen Kunstausstellung in Rom. Knapp vor Ausbruch des Ersten Weltkrieges, am 16. Mai 1914, wurde die Deutsche Werkbundausstellung in Köln eröffnet, für die HOFFMANN das Österreich-Haus geschaffen hatte. Unter Mitarbeit von OSWALD HAERDTL und Max Fellerer entstand 1924/25 der Österreichische Pavillon auf der Internationalen Kunstgewerbeausstellung (Exposition Internationale des Arts Décoratifs et Industriels Modernes) 1925 in Paris. Einzelne Bauteile des von HOFFMANN dafür geschaffenen Gesamtkonzeptes schufen Peter Behrens, JOSEF FRANK und Oskar Strnad. Einen letzten

Adolf Loos, House Tzara, Paris, 1925/26

Adolf Loos, Villa Müller, Prague, 1928–30

Biennial exhibition in Venice, which he built with the cooperation of Robert Kramreiter.

Today, ADOLF LOOS **(1870 Brno/Moravia – 1933 Kalksburg/Vienna) is on equal standing with** OTTO WAGNER **as an outstanding architect. He was considered to be the moralist among the Austrian architects of the time. His Moravian descent, his restlessness, his debts, his admirers and what he considered to be his failure at the Vienna Housing Office forced him to work abroad in Moravia and France a number of times.** LOOS **lived in Paris as an "émigré" between 1924 and 1928.**

LOOS'S **first completed building is located in Switzerland. It is the Karma Villa, which he built for the Viennese Physiologist Dr. Theoder Beer between 1903 and 1906 in Clarens, close to Montreux. In 1916, in the middle of WWI, he built the sugar refinery and Villa for the facility's director at Rohrbach, close to Brno, Slovakia. In 1923, when** LOOS **was already spending a large part of the year in France, he created the design for the Villa on the Lido in Venice of Alexander Moissi, the great Austrian actor. Only the three most important projects that he completed in France deserve to be mentioned here: the Tristan Tzara House (1925/26), the Knize Men's Tailor salon (1927/28) and the house of the entertainer Josephine Baker.**

One of LOOS' **last artistic high points was the villa he created in Prague for the construction entrepreneur František Müller between 1928 and 1930. The worker's housing project in Babí close to Nachod that consisted of five buildings**

Höhepunkt der Ausstellungsbauten HOFFMANNS stellt der Österreichische Pavillon für die Biennale 1934 in Venedig dar, an dessen Ausführung Robert Kramreiter beteiligt gewesen war.

Als ähnlich herausragende Persönlichkeit wie OTTO WAGNER erscheint heute ADOLF LOOS (1870 Brünn/Mähren – 1933 Kalksburg bei Wien), der als Moralist unter den österreichischen Architekten gilt. Seine mährische Herkunft, seine Rastlosigkeit, seine chronische Verschuldung, seine Anhängerschaft und seine von ihm als gescheitert betrachtete Tätigkeit im Wiener Siedlungsamt ließen ihn wiederholt in Mähren und Frankreich tätig sein. 1924 bis 1928 lebte LOOS in der „Emigration" in Paris.

Das erste realisierte Bauwerk von LOOS entstand in der Schweiz. Es ist die 1903 bis 1906 errichtete Villa Karma in Clarens bei Montreux/Schweiz für den Wiener Physiologen Dr. Theodor Beer. Mitten im Krieg, 1916, schuf er die Zuckerraffinerie und die Villa für deren Direktor in Rohrbach bei Brünn. 1923, als LOOS schon große Teile des Jahres in Frankreich lebte, entstand der Entwurf für die Villa des großen Schauspielers Alexander Moissi für den Lido in Venedig. Von den zahlreichen für Frankreich entstandenen Projekten und ausgeführten Entwürfen seien hier nur die drei wichtigsten für Paris genannt: Haus Tristan Tzara (1925/26), Herrenmodesalon Knize (1927/28) und das Projekt für das Haus der Tänzerin Josephine Baker (1927).

Einen letzten künstlerischen Höhepunkt erreichte LOOS 1928–30 mit seiner Villa für den Bauunternehmer František Müller in Prag. 1931 entstand noch nach

Michael Rosenauer,
Arlington House,
London, 1936

Michael Rosenauer,
Time-Life-Building,
London, 1951

was built according to his designs in 1931.

MICHAEL ROSENAUER **(1884 Wels/Upper Austria – 1971 London), whose work is unjustly almost forgotten today, belongs to a generation that came after** LOOS **und** HOFFMANN**. The son of a family of construction contractors, was born in Wels/Upper Austria. In 1928, the chiefarchitect of the British Ministry of Health invited him to act as an advisor to the British government in creating housing programs. In 1930, after years of shuttling between London and Vienna,** ROSENAUER **moved to London permanently. He also built two villas near to Paris around this time: the villa for Count Paul de Vallombrosa in St. Cloud and the Chalet a Garches for the Minister François Pietri. In London,** ROSENAUER **built an apartment building on Grosvenor Square in 1936 and another on Arlington Street, which at the time of its construction was considered Europe's most modern apartment building.**

In 1940, ROSENAUER **moved to America where he first resided in Washington before moving to New York. In 1951, he was commissioned to build the European bureau building for Time-Life, the American magazine publishing group.** ROSENAUER **seized this opportunity to return to London and further developed his concept of simple, freestanding, Viennese Dorotheum-style buildings. The Westbury Hotel was built across the street from the Time-Life building according to his plans. In 1954, he built hotels on the Bahamas and the Canary Islands.**

seinen Entwürfen die aus fünf Siedlungshäusern bestehende Arbeitersiedlung in Babí bei Nachod.

Schon einer späteren Generation als LOOS und HOFFMANN gehört MICHAEL ROSENAUER (1884 Wels/Oberösterreich – 1971 London) an, der heute sehr zu unrecht nahezu vergessen ist. Er wurde 1884 in Wels/Oberösterreich als Sohn einer oberösterreichischen Baumeisterfamilie geboren. 1928 erhielt er vom Chefarchitekten des britischen Gesundheitsministeriums die Einladung, die Britische Regierung bei der Erstellung von Wohnbauprogrammen zu beraten. Nach Jahren des Pendelns zwischen London und Wien übersiedelte ROSENAUER 1930 endgültig nach London. Um diese Zeit entstanden auch zwei Villen in der Umgebung von Paris: die Villa für Count Paul de Vallombrosa in St. Cloud und das Chalet a Garches für den Minister François Pietri. In London errichtete ROSENAUER unter anderen 1936 ein Miethaus am Grosvenor Square und ein weiteres an der Arlington Street, das zu seiner Entstehungszeit als das modernste Miethaus Europas bezeichnet wurde.

1940 übersiedelte ROSENAUER nach Amerika und ließ sich vorerst in Washington und später in New York nieder. 1951 erhielt er den Auftrag für die Errichtung des europäischen Zentralverwaltungsgebäudes des amerikanischen Zeitschriftenkonzerns Time-Life in London. ROSENAUER nützte die Gelegenheit für seine Rückkehr nach London und entwickelte mit dem freistehenden Block an der Ecke New Bond Street/Bruton Street seine nach Einfachheit strebenden Konzepte der Wiener Dorotheumsbauten weiter.

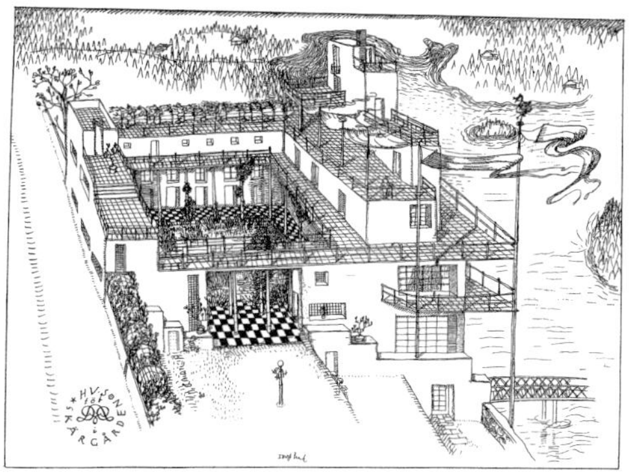

Josef Frank, Double house Weissenhofsiedlung, Stuttgart, 1925–27

Josef Frank, House for Dagmar Grill, Skärgården, 1926

JOSEF FRANK **(1885 Baden bei Wien – 1967 Stockholm) studied under Carl König at Vienna Technical University, as did** MICHAEL ROSENAUER. FRANK'S **first contract outside Austria was the construction of the Museum of East Asian Art in Cologne, which brought him into contact with East Asian, Chinese and Japanese architecture. These influences were evident in his later work.** FRANK **was the only Austrian who built a two-family residential unit for the Stuttgart Werkbund Project.**

In 1932, FRANK **came into contact with "Svenskt Tenn" ("Swedish Tin") a Swedish company based in Stockholm, for which he worked continuously between 1934 and 1966.** FRANK **left Austria in 1934 and, except for a few intervals, lived in Sweden until his death in 1967.**

He completed a number of villa projects for his chosen country before emigrating there. After 1934, he built a few single-family houses in Sweden again, such as Laftmann House, Seth House and the Wehtje House. His design work includes the 13 projected single-family houses for Dagmar Grill (1947), the Reichstag Parliament expansion project in Stockholm (1950) and the plans for the four "D-Houses" (1953). He also drafted a number of designs for projects in America.

CLEMENS HOLZMEISTER
(1886 Fulpmes/Tyrol – 1983 Hallein/Salzburg) was another Vienna Technical University graduate. His pupils – Holzmeister-Schüler – GUSTAV PEICHL, WILHELM HOLZBAUER, HANS HOLLEIN **and many others) made him a household name,**

Gegenüber dem Time-Life-Building entstand nach seinen Plänen das Westbury Hotel. Um 1954 errichtete er Hotels auf den Bahamas und den Kanarischen Inseln.

Wie MICHAEL ROSENAUER studierte auch JOSEF FRANK (1885 Baden bei Wien – 1967 Stockholm) an der Technischen Hochschule in Wien bei Carl König. FRANKS erster Auftrag außerhalb Österreichs war 1912 die Einrichtung des Museums für Ostasiatische Kunst in Köln, die ihn mit der Architektur Ostasiens, Chinas und Japans in Kontakt brachte, von der er bei den nachfolgenden Bauten beeinflusst werden sollte. In der Werkbundsiedlung in Stuttgart führte FRANK als einziger österreichischer Vertreter ein Doppelwohnhaus aus.

1932 kam es zum ersten Kontakt FRANKS mit der Firma „Svenskt Tenn" („Schwedisches Zinn") in Stockholm, für die er zwischen 1934 und 1966 ständig arbeiten sollte. 1934 verließ FRANK Österreich und lebte mit kurzen Unterbrechungen bis zu seinem Tod 1967 in Schweden.

Bereits vor seiner Emigration nach Schweden errichtete er zahlreiche Villenprojekte für seine spätere zweite Heimat. Nach 1934 konnte er erneut einige Einfamilienhäuser in Schweden realisieren, wie beispielsweise das Haus Laftmann, das Haus Seth und das Haus Wehtje. An Entwürfen sind noch die 13 projektierten Einfamilienhäuser für Dagmar Grill (1947), das Projekt für die Erweiterung des Reichstagsgebäudes in Stockholm (1950) und die Entwürfe für vier „D-Houses"

Clemens Holzmeister, St. Adalbert, Berlin, 1930–33

Clemens Holzmeister, Hotel Tre Cime, Sexten-Moos, Southern Tyrol, 1926

and he had great influence on architecture in and from Austria today. Since he was a Brazilian citizen due to his father's emigration to that country earlier, he was not drafted and worked at the Vienna Technical University as an assistant during WWI. He was a professor at the Academy of Art in Düsseldorf from 1928 until 1933. In1938, Holzmeister was forced to retire as the director of the special architecture school of the Academy of Fine Arts in Vienna. He chose Turkey as his exile until 1947. In Turkey, he was introduced to the Turkish Leader Atatürk and was able to complete large state projects. He taught at Istanbul Technical University from 1940 until 1949. In 1954, Holzmeister was recalled to "his" Master School of the Academy of Fine Arts in Vienna as a professor without seniority and he returned to Vienna permanently.

Only a few of the around 700 projects that are mentioned in Clemens Holzmeister's project list can be named here: St. Martin's Church in Nuremberg/Germany (1926–35), Hotel Drei Zinnen (Tre Cime, Three Towers) in Sexten-Moos/Southern Tyrol, Italy (1926), St.Peter Parish Church in Mönchengladbach-Waldhausen/Germany (1928–33), the Schlageter Memorial in Golzheimer Heide near Düsseldorf/Germany (1929–31), the Maria-Grün Parish Church in Hamburg/Germany (1929/30), St. Adalbert Church in Berlin/Germany (1930–33), Christkönigs-Church in Meran/Southern Tyrol, Italy (1930–36), Christkönigs-Church (St. Elisabeth) in Kleve/Germany (1932–34), Trebitsch House in Dubrovnik/Croatia (1932/33), the Klemens-Hofbauer Church

(1953) aufzuzählen. Darüber hinaus entstanden auch zahlreiche Entwürfe für Amerika.

Gleichfalls ein Absolvent der Technischen Hochschule in Wien war CLEMENS HOLZMEISTER (1886 Fulpmes/Tirol – 1983 Hallein/Salzburg). Durch seine Schüler – „Holzmeister-Schüler" ist heute ein bekannter Begriff (GUSTAV PEICHL, WILHELM HOLZBAUER, HANS HOLLEIN u.v.a.) – ist er von größtem Einfluss auf die heutige Architektur in Österreich und vor allem „aus" Österreich. Da er durch seinen Vater brasilianischer Staatsbürger war, musste er nicht einrücken und war während des Ersten Weltkrieges als Assistent an der TH Wien tätig. 1928 bis 1933 übernahm er ein Lehramt an der Kunstakademie in Düsseldorf. 1938 wurde HOLZMEISTER als Leiter einer Spezialschule für Architektur an der Akademie der bildenden Künste in Wien zwangspensioniert. Als Exil wählte er bis 1947 die Türkei, wo er mit Atatürk bekannt wurde und große staatliche Aufträge ausführen konnte. Von 1940 bis 1949 lehrte er an der Technischen Universität Istanbul. Mit der 1954 erfolgten Rückberufung als Ordinarius an „seine" Meisterschule an der Akademie der bildenden Künste in Wien, gab er seinen Wohnsitz in der Türkei endgültig auf.

Aus dem rund 700 Nummern umfassenden Werkverzeichnis von CLEMENS HOLZMEISTER mit zahlreichen Bauten und Projekten für Europa können hier nur einige der wesentlichsten Bauten genannt werden: St. Martin in Nürnberg/Deutschland (1926–35), Hotel Drei Zinnen (Tre Cime) in Sexten-Moos/Südtirol (1926), Pfarrkirche St. Petrus in Mönchenglad-

Lois Welzenbacher, House Settari, Bad Dreikirchen, Southern Tyrol, 1922/23

Lois Welzenbacher, House Schulz, Recklinghausen, 1928/29

in Hodonice/Czech Republic (1932/33) and the "Twelve Apostles" Parish Church including a parish and youth home in Augsburg/Germany (1961–67).

LOIS WELZENBACHER **and** FRIEDRICH KIESLER **are two particularly unique individualists whose work differed greatly, but they nonetheless deserve mention here.**

LOIS WELZENBACHER **(1889 Munich – 1955 Absam/Tyrol) was born in Munich as his father, a stonemason, moved to the Bavarian city at the end of the 19th century, but he retained his Austrian citizenship.** WELZENBACHER **only began his architecture studies at the Bavarian Technical University in Munich in 1912.**

In 1929, WELZENBACHER **became the Director of Urban Construction in Plauen. In 1931, he opened a studio in Munich, in addition to a studio in Innsbruck. He acted as a consulting architect for the aircraft production plant in Halle an der Saale, Germany, from 1939 until 1942.**

WELZENBACHER'S **strong German nexus naturally had an effect on his work. But along with the buildings and projects in Germany, he also submitted a large number of entries for competitions in other European countries. Only a few of the most important buildings can be listed here: Mimi Settari House in Bad Dreikirchen close to Waidbruck/Southern Tyrol (1922/23), Schulz House in Recklinghausen/Germany (1928/29), Terrassenhotel am Oberjoch in Allgäu/Germany (1932/33), the Ehlert Children's Home School in Hindelang-Allgäu/Germany (1934), Welzenbacher House in Munich/Germany (1935), Hotel**

bach-Waldhausen/Deutschland (1928–33), Schlageter-Denkmal in der Golzheimer Heide bei Düsseldorf/Deutschland (1929–31), Pfarrkirche Maria-Grün in Hamburg/Deutschland (1929/30), St. Adalbert in Berlin/Deutschland (1930–33), Christkönigskirche in Meran/Südtirol (1930–36), Christkönigskirche (St. Elisabeth) in Kleve/Deutschland (1932–34), Haus Trebitsch in Dubrovnik/Kroatien (1932/33), Klemens-Hofbauer-Kirche in Hodonice/Tschechische Republik (1932/33), Pfarrkirche „Zwölf Apostel" mit Pfarr- und Jugendheim in Augsburg/Deutschland (1961–67).

Mit LOIS WELZENBACHER und FRIEDRICH KIESLER werden im folgenden zwei besonders eigenwillige aber auch voneinander sehr unterschiedliche Individualisten genannt.

LOIS WELZENBACHER (1889 München - 1955 Absam/Tirol) kam in München zur Welt, da sein Vater Ende des 19. Jahrhunderts als Steinmetz in die bayrische Metropole übersiedelt war, um dort zu arbeiten, jedoch die österreichische Staatsbürgerschaft beibehalten hatte. Erst 1912 begann WELZENBACHER als österreichischer Staatsbürger sein Architekturstudium an der Bayrischen Technischen Hochschule in München.

1929 wurde WELZENBACHER Stadtbaudirektor in Plauen. 1931 eröffnete er zusätzlich zu seinem Atelier in Innsbruck ein Atelier in München. Von 1939 bis 1942 war er beratender Architekt der Flugzeugwerke in Halle an der Saale.

Der durch seine Biographie sich ergebende starke Bezug WELZENBACHERS zu Deutschland schlägt sich naturgemäß auch in seinem Werk nieder. Neben

Friedrich Kiesler, Theater Exhibition for the "Exposition Internationale des Arts Décoratifs et Industriels Modernes", Paris, 1925

am Lautersee in Mittenwald/Upper Bavaria (1935), the leather factory, residential unit, staff quarters, gate keeper's house and workers quarters in Ranz-Schonbau/Allgäu/Germany (1936–38), the Siebel aircraft plant in Halle an der Saale/Germany (1939–44).

FRIEDRICH KIESLER'S **(1890 Czernowitz/Bukowina – 1965 New York) focus was entirely different. Today, he is internationally recognized as a leading Austrian avant-garde architect. He was in Berlin a number of times between 1921 and 1922, where he designed the sets for R.U.R., a play by Karl Czapek. In 1924, Kiesler created the sets for Eugene O'Neill's play "The Emperor Jones" in Berlin. He was invited to design the Austrian theater section of the 1925 Paris Exposition Internationale des Arts Décoratifs et Industrials by** JOSEF HOFFMANN. **For a hall of the Grand Palais,** KIESLER **built a futuristic Raumstadt: a monumental spatial structure in the style of De Stijl, in which he integrated stage models, theater designs and costume designs by Austrian architects and artists. He created more architectural concepts in Paris, where he proposed the "horizontal skyscrapers," as well as a project for the re-design of the Place de la Concorde.**

At the beginning of 1926, he traveled to New York on an ocean liner with materials to mount an exhibition. What was intended as a visit and participation in an exhibition became led to KIESLER'S **staying in New York for the rest of his life. From 1957 until his death in 1965 the architect worked on the, "Shrine of the Book," in Jerusalem, in which the**

Bauten und Projekten für Deutschland entstanden jedoch noch zahlreiche Wettbewerbsprojekte für andere europäische Länder. Es können hier nur einige der wichtigsten Bauten aufgelistet werden: Haus Mimi Settari in Bad Dreikirchen bei Waidbruck/Südtirol (1922/23), Haus Schulz in Recklinghausen/Deutschland (1928/29), Terrassenhotel am Oberjoch im Allgäu/Deutschland (1932/33), Schule zum Kinderheim Ehlert in Hindelang-Allgäu/Deutschland (1934), Haus Welzenbacher in München/Deutschland (1935), Hotel am Lautersee in Mittenwald/Oberbayern (1935), Lederfabrik mit Wohnhaus, Gefolgschaftshaus, Pförtnerhaus und Arbeiterwohnhaus in Ranz-Schonbau/Allgäu (1936–38), Flugzeugwerke Siebel in Halle an der Saale/Deutschland (1939–44).

Gänzlich anders ist die Interessenslage von FRIEDRICH KIESLER (1890 Czernowitz/Bukowina – 1965 New York), dem heute international anerkannten Avantgardearchitekten Österreichs. 1921 und 1922 hielt er sich wiederholt in Berlin auf, wo er 1923 das Bühnenbild für das Theaterstück R.U.R. von Karl Czapek gestaltete. 1924 arbeitete KIESLER an dem Bühnenbild für Eugen O'Neills Stück „The Emperor Jones" für Berlin. 1925 wurde er von JOSEF HOFFMANN eingeladen, die österreichische Theaterabteilung der Pariser Exposition Internationale des Arts Décoratifs et Industriels Modernes zu gestalten. Für einen Saal des Grand Palais baute KIESLER seine futuristische „Raumstadt": eine monumentale, im Stil von De Stijl gehaltene, räumliche Struktur, in welche er Bühnenmodelle, Theaterpläne und Kostüment-

Franz Schuster, Administration Building Disch AG, Frankfurt, 1928–29

Franz Schuster, Settlement Römerstadt, Frankfurt, 1927–30

Dead Sea Scrolls are on display from 1957 until his death in 1965. It is the only project of KIESLER'S **that was actually completed.**

FRANZ SCHUSTER **(1892 Vienna – 1972 Vienna) can be considered one of Austria's most important architects of the post WWII period along with** LOIS WELZENBACHER. **In the twenties he worked at the Frankfurt am Main Building Department with** ANTON BRENNER **and** MARGARETE SCHÜTTE-LIHOTZKY. **After attending the Vienna Arts and Crafts School,** SCHUSTER **moved to Dresden-Hellerau, were he worked at Heinrich Tessenow's office until 1922. He completed his first project as a freelance architect in 1923, when he built the studio house for Professor Petrich in Hellerau. He returned to Vienna the same year. After various activities in Vienna, he moved to Frankfurt am Main at the request of City Councilman Ernst May in 1927. He was appointed professor of Special Residential Construction and Interior Decoration at the Frankfurt (Städelschule) School of Arts and Crafts in 1928 and remained there until 1933. He also held guest lectures at the Royal Academy in Copenhagen before being named Senior Professor of the Special Architecture Class of the Vienna School of Arts and Crafts in 1937.**

After accepting his appointment in Frankfurt, SCHUSTER **was able to build a number of remarkable buildings and housing projects there, such as the Römerstadt Project (Roman City). His publishing activities also flourished parallel to these activities. Among** SCHUSTERS' **administration buildings the**

würfe österreichischer Architekten und Künstler integrierte. In Paris entwarf er weitere Architekturkonzepte, wie beispielsweise die „horizontalen Wolkenkratzer" sowie ein Projekt zur Umgestaltung des Place de la Concorde.

Anfang 1926 reiste KIESLER mit Ausstellungsmaterial per Schiff nach New York. Aus dem geplanten Besuch für eine Ausstellungsbeteiligung wurde aber ein bis an sein Lebensende währender Aufenthalt. Von 1957 bis zu seinem Tod 1965 arbeitete er an seinem einzigen tatsächlich realisierten Bauwerk: dem „Shrine of the Book" für Jerusalem, in dem die Schriftrollen vom Toten Meer ausgestellt sind.

Wie LOIS WELZENBACHER zählt FRANZ SCHUSTER (1892 Wien – 1972 Wien) zu den wichtigen Nachkriegsarchitekten Österreichs. In den zwanziger Jahren war er gemeinsam mit ANTON BRENNER und MARGARETE SCHÜTTE-LIHOTZKY am Hochbauamt in Frankfurt am Main tätig. Nach Besuch der Wiener Kunstgewerbeschule übersiedelte SCHUSTER nach Dresden-Hellerau, wo er im Architekturbüro Heinrich Tessenows bis 1922 arbeitete. Als selbstständiger Architekt realisierte er 1923 mit dem „Atelierhaus" für Professor Petrich in Hellerau sein erstes Bauvorhaben. Im selben Jahr kehrte er nach Wien zurück. Nach unterschiedlichen Tätigkeiten in Wien übersiedelte er auf Aufforderung des Stadtrates für Bauwesen Ernst May 1927 nach Frankfurt am Main. Dort wurde er 1928 an die Kunstgewerbeschule (Städelschule) als Leiter der Fachklasse für Wohnungsbau und Innenausstattung berufen, wo er bis 1933 tätig war. 1932 hielt er Gastvorle-

Anton Brenner, Praunheim Housing Project, Frankfurt, 1928

Disch AG (1928–1929) deserves mention here. One of his most important projects during his years in Frankfurt was the Opel-Bad swimming pool in Wiesbaden.

After the end of WWII, FRANZ SCHUSTER **mainly spent his time in Austria and was mostly employed in Vienna. The studio house he built for Dr. Schenk in 1954 in Darmstadt was one of the last of his projects to be completed in Germany. He also built the Nordweststadt in Frankfurt in 1961. A psychological care center was built according to his plans in Thessaloniki, Northern Greece at around the same time.**

ANTON BRENNER **(1896 Vienna – 1957 Frauenkirchen, Burgenland, Austria) is almost as forgotten as** MICHAEL ROSENAUER. **He was taken prisoner by the Russians in 1916 where he received his first technical training from fellow prisoners of war such as Hans Jaksch. After an adventurous escape, he built a Protestant church and school in Tsingtau/China in 1920. In 1924, he won a residential building project competition initiated by the Berlin Periodical "Bauwelt" (Construction World). Worn down by the intrigues in Vienna, he moved to Frankfurt am Main at the end of 1926, where he worked at the City Building Department. As an associate to Ernst May (whom he accused of all imaginable forms of negative characteristics as a person in his pamphlet "Mit Ach und Krach durchs Leben", Making My Way Through Life painfully) he designed apartments for terraced housing in Frankfurt-Praunheim and the floor plans for the Emittiertensiedlung Project on Mammolshainerstraße in Frankfurt.**

sungen an der Königlichen Akademie in Kopenhagen. 1937 erfolgte seine Berufung an die Kunstgewerbeschule in Wien als Leiter der Fachklasse für Architektur.

Durch seine Berufung nach Frankfurt am Main konnte SCHUSTER hier eine Reihe von bemerkenswerten Bauten und Siedlungsanlagen errichten, so zum Beispiel 1927 die Siedlung „Römerstadt". Daneben nahm er seine publizistische Tätigkeit auf. Von SCHUSTERS Verwaltungsbauten in Frankfurt ist das Bürohaus für die Disch AG (1928–29) zu nennen. Zu den Hauptwerken seiner Frankfurter Zeit zählt das 1932 errichtete Opel-Bad in Wiesbaden.

Nach dem Ende des Zweiten Weltkrieges war FRANZ SCHUSTER hauptsächlich in Österreich und hier vor allem in Wien tätig. Zu den wenigen Bauten, die er noch in Deutschland errichtete, zählt das Atelierhaus für Dr. Schenk in Darmstadt von 1954. 1961 errichtete er in Frankfurt die „Nordweststadt". Etwa zur gleichen Zeit entstand nach seinen Plänen in Thessaloniki in Nordgriechenland ein psychologisches Zentrum

Mindestens so vergessen wie MICHAEL ROSENAUER ist ANTON BRENNER (1896 Wien – 1957 Frauenkirchen/Burgenland). Er geriet 1916 in russische Kriegsgefangenschaft, wo er durch Mitgefangene (u. a. durch Hans Jaksch) seinen ersten technischen Unterricht erhielt. Nach einer abenteuerlichen Flucht erbaute er 1920 in Tsingtau/China eine protestantische Kirche und eine Schule. 1924 ging BRENNER siegreich aus einem Wohnhauswettbewerb der Berliner Zeitschrift „Bauwelt" hervor. Zermürbt von zahllosen Intrigen in Wien wechselte er Ende 1926 nach

Anton Brenner, Terraced Housing, Wannseebahn, Berlin, 1928

Margarete Lihotzky, Frankfurt Kitchen, Frankfurt, 1927

In 1928, BRENNER **planned and built a building with deciduous trees in Frankfurt-Praunheim ("Brennerblock"), for which he coined the maxim, "living the sanatorium lifestyle." Due to yet another intrigue, he was forced to build another building with deciduous trees in Berlin-Wannseebahn the same year, instead of building it alone as intended, he had to build it in cooperation with the architects Mebes & Emmerich. He was invited to join the Bauhaus effort in Dessau the following year, but he was once again disappointed by his students and colleagues, and left again a few months later. After the end of the war, he designed the British Embassy in Vienna, before accepting a chair as a professor in India in 1951 at the Indian Institute of Technology. Deeply depressed by the unsatisfactory living conditions there, he returned to Austria in 1953.**

MARGARETE LIHOTZKY **(1897 Vienna – 2000 Vienna) accepted a job as an architect under Vermeer in Holland after completing her studies at the Vienna School of Arts and Crafts. Ernst May invited her to join the Frankfurt Building Department in 1926, where she focused on the rationalization of building economics and the implementation of such measures in residential construction. Her most famous work during this period was the Frankfurter Küche, (The Frankfurt Kitchen). Since she married the architect Wilhelm Schütte in 1927, and cost-cutting measures applied to double-income couples, her contract at the Frankfurt Building Department was not renewed. Hence she and her husband submitted a number of joint com-**

Frankfurt am Main ins Hochbauamt. Als Mitarbeiter von Ernst May (dem er in seinem Typoskript „Mit Ach und Krach durchs Leben" alle nur erdenklichen schlechten menschlichen Eigenschaften nachsagte) entwarf er Einliegerwohnungen für Reihenhäuser in Frankfurt-Praunheim sowie die Grundrisse der Emittiertensiedlung in der Frankfurter Mammolshainerstraße. 1928 plante und baute BRENNER das Laubenganghaus in Frankfurt-Praunheim („Brennerblock"), für das er das Motto „wohnen wie im Sanatorium" prägte. Aufgrund einer neuerlichen Intrige musste er gemeinsam – und nicht wie ursprünglich beabsichtigt alleine – mit den Architekten Mebes & Emmerich im selben Jahr das Laubenganghaus in Berlin-Wannseebahn errichten. Im Jahr darauf berief ihn Hannes Mayer ans Bauhaus in Dessau, das er aber einige Monate später – erneut menschlich von seinen Studenten und Meisterkollegen enttäuscht – wieder verließ. Nach Kriegsende plante er für die Englische Botschaft in Wien. 1951 erfolgte seine Berufung als Professor nach Indien an das „Indian Institute of Technology". Tief deprimiert von den dortigen unzulänglichen Lebensbedingungen kehrte er 1953 nach Österreich zurück.

MARGARETE LIHOTZKY (1897 Wien – 2000 Wien) war nach Abschluss ihres Studiums an der Wiener Kunstgewerbeschule 1920 bei Architekt Vermeer in Holland tätig. 1926 berief sie Ernst May in das Hochbauamt der Stadt Frankfurt, wo sie sich mit der Rationalisierung der Hauswirtschaft und ihrer Umsetzung im Wohnbau beschäftigte. Ihre bekannteste

Oswald Haerdtl, Austrian Pavilion World Fair, Brussels, 1935

Oswald Haerdtl, Austrian Pavilion World Fair, Paris, 1937

petition entries. In 1930, MARGARETE SCHÜTTE-LIHOTZKY **was asked to join the May Group for the planning of new cities in Moscow. She was an employee at the Architecture Academy in Moscow from 1934 to 1936. An adventurous phase in her life led her to Stalingrad, Odessa, Istanbul, Athens, Trieste, Paris, London and Berlin over the next years. In Berlin, she was arrested by the Gestapo and sentenced to 15 years in prison. After her liberation by American troops in 1945, she made her way to Sofia, Bulgaria, arriving there in 1946. In Sofia, she worked on children's facilities at the City Building Department before finally returning to Vienna in 1947.**

One of JOSEF HOFFMANN'S **associates was** OSWALD HAERDTL **(1899 Vienna – 1959 Vienna), who was also a professor at the University of Applied of Arts for many years. His teaching and construction activities as well as his international connections, especially in Italy and France, made it possible for** HAERDTL **to ensure the continuity of classical Viennese modernism in the years of reconstruction after the war.**

Internationally, he was the architect responsible for the Austrian Pavilions at the World Fair in Brussels in 1935 and in Paris in 1937. The light, playfully elegant forms employed, characterized these designs. But he was also responsible for other projects beyond Austria's borders. In 1925, he contributed a "garden room" construction and the "office foyers" to the Austrian pavilion at the 1925 Exposition des Arts Décoratifs. A house for a religious order was built according to his plans in Cluj (Klausenburg) Romania

Arbeit aus dieser Zeit ist die „Frankfurter Küche". Da sie 1927 den Architekten WILHELM SCHÜTTE geheiratet hatte, wurde wegen Personaleinsparungsmaßnahmen bei Doppelverdienern 1929 ihr Vertrag am Frankfurter Hochbauamt nicht mehr verlängert. Sie beteiligte sich daher gemeinsam mit ihrem Mann an mehreren Wettbewerben. 1930 wurde MARGARETE SCHÜTTE-LIHOTZKY als Mitglied der Gruppe May für die Planung neuer Städte nach Moskau berufen. Von 1934 bis 1936 war sie Mitarbeiterin der Architekturakademie in Moskau. Ein abenteuerliches Leben führte sie in den kommenden Jahren unter anderem nach Stalingrad, Odessa, Istanbul, Athen, Triest, Paris, London und Berlin, wo sie von der Gestapo verhaftet zu fünfzehn Jahren Zuchthaus verurteilt wurde. Nach der Befreiung 1945 durch amerikanische Truppen gelangte sie 1946 nach Sofia in Bulgarien, wo sie für Kindereinrichtungen am Stadtbauamt beschäftigt war. 1947 kehrte sie endgültig nach Wien zurück.

Ein Mitarbeiter JOSEF HOFFMANNS und wie dieser langjährig Professor an der Hochschule für angewandte Kunst war OSWALD HAERDTL (1899 Wien – 1959 Wien). Mit seiner Lehre und Bautätigkeit sowie durch internationale Verbindungen, besonders nach Italien und Frankreich, ermöglichte HAERDTL die Kontinuität der klassischen Wiener Moderne in den Jahren des Wiederaufbaus der Nachkriegszeit.

International trat er als Architekt der österreichischen Pavillons auf den Weltausstellungen in Brüssel 1935 und in Paris 1937 hervor, in denen er eine

Roland Rainer, Multi-Purpose Hall, Bremen, 1955–65

Roland Rainer, Garden Courtyard House, Kassel, 1979–82

in 1926. From 1941 until 1944 HAERDTL **built the Park Hotel in Krakow. He designed the interiors of the Austrian Mission building in Moscow in 1949.**

The first architect named here who was born in the 20th century is ROLAND RAINER. **He was born in 1910 in Klagenfurt/Carinthia. He went to Berlin in 1936, where he worked at the Academy for Urban Construction until 1939. After his service in the German Wehrmacht (1939–1945), he settled in Vienna and worked as an architect. In 1956, after teaching at the Hannover and Graz Technical University** RAINER **was appointed the head of the Architecture Master Class at the Academy of Fine Arts in Vienna. He exercised this function until 1980. He was also responsible for urban planning in Vienna from 1958 until 1963.**

RAINER **developed coherent teachings covering everything from individual houses to urban construction projects in a number of publications. He was a proponent of living close to nature in dense, low-surface buildings and revived antique ideas such atriums and absorbed influences from the orient (e.g. the Linz Gartenstadt, Garden City, in Puchenau, 1966–1982).** RAINER **made use of an expressive-constructive language to express democratic representation in his large public projects. Aside for the Vienna Stadthalle Event Hall (1955–58), he also built multi-purpose halls in Bremen (1955–65) and the Stadthalle Event Hall in Ludwigshafen (1962–65). Rainer also designed the interiors for his public buildings. His publications cover a broad scope of themes ranging from the**

leichte, spielerisch-elegante Formensprache zeigte. Darüber hinaus entstanden aber noch andere Werke außerhalb der Grenzen Österreichs. Mit der Einrichtung eines „Gartenzimmers" und dem „Vorraum der Büros" beteiligte er sich 1925 im österreichischen Pavillon an der Exposition des Arts Décoratifs in Paris. 1936 entstand in Cluj (Klausenburg) in Rumänien das Stammhaus der Sozialen Schwestern nach seinen Plänen. 1941 bis 1944 erbaute HAERDTL in Krakau das Parkhotel. Die österreichische Gesandtschaft in Moskau richtete er 1949 ein.

Der erste hier genannte Architekt, der im 20. Jahrhundert auf die Welt kam, ist ROLAND RAINER. Er wurde 1910 in Klagenfurt/Kärnten geboren.1936 ging er nach Berlin, wo er bis 1939 an der Städtebau-Akademie arbeitete. Nach den Jahren als Angehöriger der Deutschen Wehrmacht (1939–1945) ließ er sich in Wien als Architekt nieder. Nach Unterrichtstätigkeiten an den Technischen Hochschulen in Hannover und Graz wurde RAINER 1956 als Leiter der Meisterschule für Architektur an die Akademie der bildenden Künste in Wien berufen. Diese Funktion hatte er bis 1980 inne. Von 1958 bis 1963 war RAINER Stadtplaner von Wien.

RAINER entwickelte in zahlreichen Publikationen eine zusammenhängende Lehre vom Einzelhaus bis zum Städtebau. Für Privathäuser propagierte er das naturnahe Wohnen im verdichteten Flachbau und griff Ideen aus der Antike (Atriumhaus) und dem Orient auf (z. B. Gartenstadt Puchenau bei Linz, 1966–82). Für seine großen öffentlichen Bauten verwendete RAINER eine expressiv-

Karl Schwanzer, BMW Administration Building, Munich, 1973

Günther Domenig, Pavilion for the Olympic Swimming Hall, Munich, 1970–72

discussion of residential and urban construction issues to views on the adequate outer spaces and gardens or anonymous constructions. The study of other cultures was also the subject of a number of publications.

In 1982, RAINER **participated in the "documenta urbana" exhibition in Kassel with an impressive garden courtyard house model.**

KARL SCHWANZER **(1918 Vienna – 1975 Vienna) is an architect whose work merits a comprehensive study and reorganization. He achieved international recognition quickly and taught as a visiting professor at a number of technical universities such as those in Dortmund (1964/65), Budapest (1967) and Darmstadt (1973). In 1958, he created the Austrian pavilion for he World Fair in Brussels, which was transferred to the Swiss Gardens in Vienna and opened as the "Museum of the 20th Century" in 1962.** SCHWANZER **also designed the pavilion of the European Council for the 1967 World Fair. He designed the Zwiebelhaus (Onion House) in Munich in 1970. In 1971, he built the BMW parking building in Munich with prefabricated components. In 1973, he added the BMW administration building and the corresponding museum to the facility. These are** SCHWANZER'S **most important projects outside of Austria.**

GÜNTHER DOMENIG **built the pavilion for the Olympic Swimming Hall in Munich for the games in 1972.**

Among HANS HOLLEINS' **many projects abroad, the Abteiberg City Museum in Mönchengladbach (1974–82) deserves**

konstruktive Sprache als Ausdruck demokratischer Repräsentation. Außer der Stadthalle in Wien (1955–58) schuf er die Mehrzweckhalle in Bremen (1955–65) und die Stadthalle in Ludwigshafen (1962–65). Für seine öffentlichen Bauten entwarf RAINER auch die Innenausstattungen. Seine Publikationen umfassen eine thematische Breite, die von der Auseinandersetzung mit Wohnungs- und Städtebaufragen bis hin zu Ansichten zum lebensgerechten Außenraum und Gärten oder dem anonymen Bauen reicht. Auch die Beschäftigung mit anderen Kulturen ist Thema einiger Veröffentlichungen.

1982 beteiligte sich RAINER mit einem aufsehenerregenden Gartenhofhaus an der „documenta urbana" in Kassel.

Ein Architekt, dessen Werk einer umfassenden Aufarbeitung und Neueinordnung bedürfen würde, ist KARL SCHWANZER (1918 Wien – 1975 Wien). Bald international anerkannt, unterrichtete er als Gastprofessor an mehreren technischen Hochschulen, wie z. B. in Dortmund (1964/65), Budapest (1967) und Darmstadt (1973). 1958 schuf er den Österreich-Pavillon für die Weltausstellung in Brüssel, der nach Beendigung der Ausstellung nach Wien in den Schweizergarten übertragen wurde, wo er 1962 als „Museum des 20. Jahrhunderts" eröffnet wurde. Gleichfalls für die Weltausstellung in Brüssel schuf SCHWANZER auch den Europarat-Pavillon. Für die Weltausstellung 1967 in Montreal entwarf er den Österreich-Pavillon. Für München projektierte er 1970 das Zwiebelhaus. 1971 errichtete er in München das BMW-Parkhaus aus

Hans Hollein, Abteiberg City Museum, Mönchengladbach, 1974–82

Wilhelm Holzbauer, City Hall and Opera, Amsterdam, 1979–88

special mention here.

WILHELM HOLZBAUER **began work on the City Hall and Opera in Amsterdam as early as 1979. It was completed in 1988.**

GUSTAV PEICHL **built a phosphate elimination plant in Berlin-Tegel between 1980 and 1985, the time right before the period in which the buildings that are discussed in greater depth in the following section.**

Fertigteilen. 1973 entstand mit dem BMW-Verwaltungsgebäude und dem dazugehörigen BMW-Museum in München SCHWANZERS bedeutendster Bau außerhalb Österreichs.

GÜNTHER DOMENIG errichtete 1970–72 den Pavillon der Schwimmhalle für die Olympischen Spiele in München 1972.

Von der langen Liste von Bauten HANS HOLLEINS im Ausland ist hier das Städtische Museum Abteiberg in Mönchengladbach (1974–82) zu nennen.

Bereits 1979 begann WILHELM HOLZBAUER am Rat- und Opernhaus in Amsterdam zu arbeiten, das 1988 fertiggestellt wurde.

An der zeitlichen Grenze zu den im folgenden Abschnitt ausführlich behandelten Bauten errichtete GUSTAV PEICHL in Europa die Phosphateliminationsanlage in Berlin-Tegel (1980–85).

Gustav Peichl, Phosphate Elimination Plant, Berlin-Tegel, 1980–85

export 1980—2002

1980–1985
IBA Residential Project (Internationale Bauausstellung)
Berlin-Kreuzberg, Germany
Wilhelm Holzbauer

Wilhelm Holzbauer built his programmatic Wohnen Morgen (Living Tomorrow) building in Vienna between 1973 and 1979. The goal was to offer an adequate alternative for contemporary living in a residential area with buildings from the late 19th century. Together with Jan and Rolf Rave, he created variations of this program in Berlin-Kreuzberg between 1980 and 1985. The project is on the corner of Reichenbergstraße/Mariannengasse and was intended for the International Building Exhibition. The idea was to test the concept that had been developed for Vienna under different urban construction conditions and in a location with different characteristics.

The design of the large, triangular interior courtyard was part of the construction objectives. The man-made hill with the playhouse on top and the ring of trees surrounding it makes the walls opposite to it seem larger and changes the contours. Different types of apartments are available in the complex, as was the case with the Viennese project.

The buildings have redbrick façades and white plaster walls. The brick walls of the corner house and of the secondary blocks are decorated with geometrical patterns made of blue-glazed clinker bricks, that are reminiscent of some of the traditional, especially beautiful façades and interior courtyards in the Kreuzberg area.

A network of expanded metal grids protects the entire length and height of the two buildings' double-level walkways lined with deciduous trees. The plants that grow out of troughs here cover the metal mesh, thus creating a "green architrave."

Wilhelm Holzbauer errichtete 1973-79 in Wien das programmatische Wohnhaus „Wohnen morgen". Es ging dabei um eine adäquate Alternative für das heutige Wohnen in einem im späten 19. Jahrhundert verbauten Wohngebiet. Zwischen 1980 und 1985 variierte er dieses Programm gemeinsam mit Jan und Rolf Rave in Berlin-Kreuzberg, Ecke Reichenbergstraße/Mariannengasse, für die Internationale Bauausstellung. Dabei sollte das für Wien entwickelte Konzept in einer veränderten städtebaulichen Situation und Charakteristik des „Ortes" getestet werden.

Die Gestaltung des großen, dreieckigen Innenhofes war Teil der Bauaufgabe. Der in der Mitte zugeschüttete Hügel mit einem Spielhaus und einem Ring von Bäumen lässt die Distanz zu den gegenüberliegenden Hauswänden größer erscheinen und verändert deren Konturen. Wie im Wiener Projekt stehen auch in dieser Wohnhausanlage verschiedene Wohnungstypen zur Verfügung.

Die Fassaden bestehen aus Backstein und weiß verputzten Wänden. Die Ziegelwände des Eckhauses und der Sekundärstiegenhäuser sind durch geometrische Muster aus blauglasierten Klinkern dekoriert – in Erinnerung an eine Tradition, die vor allem in Kreuzberg einige besonders schöne gestaltete Fassaden und Innenhöfe hinterließ.

Die zweigeschossigen Laubengänge der beiden Baublöcke sind über die gesamte Länge und Höhe durch ein Netzwerk aus Streckmetall geschützt; in Trögen wachsende Pflanzen überziehen das Metallgitter und formen so einen „grünen Architrav".

Round window over the entrance

Corner view

Corner view

View of the courtyard

Entrance section of the streetside façade

1980–1989
St. Judas Thaddeus Catholic Parish Church
Neureut/Karlsruhe, Germany
Ottokar Uhl

The oppressive lack of space in the rectory in the old part of Neureut, which was the result of the relocation of many of those who had been forced to move away during the war during the fifties, forced the Catholic community to search for a new church site as of 1963. However, the competition was only announced in 1980 and Ottokar Uhl's entry was selected. Financial difficulties delayed construction until 1988 and the building was christened in 1989.

The church is a simple, restrained structure. The parish residence and kindergarten are connected to it along the pedestrian path. The calming effect of the space and its walls is due to the façade material, a light grey, carefully tooled stone cement, and the few openings. The building dominates the market place across from it with its slender form and simple materials, not with mass.

Uhl remained consciously aloof from any form of aestheticism here, just as as he did in all his other buildings. His objective is to put the religious congregation at the center of his architectural considerations and to enable interior communication at a democratic level.

Uhl formulated his "church dreams" when he handed in the keys of the building: *"I imagned that this house would be a place of ideas, of discussion and of open, unrestrained criticism, also of the church."*

Die bedrückende Raumnot im Pfarrsaal des alten Ortsteiles von Neureut, die durch die Ansiedlung von Heimatvertriebenen Anfang der fünfziger Jahre des 20. Jahrhunderts entstanden war, ließ die Katholiken ab 1963 einen Bauplatz für eine Kirche suchen. Doch erst 1980 wurde ein Wettbewerb dafür ausgeschrieben, den Ottokar Uhl gewann. Finanzielle Schwierigkeiten verzögerten den Baubeginn jedoch bis 1988. 1989 konnte der Bau geweiht werden.

Die Kirche präsentiert sich als einfaches, zurückhaltendes Bauwerk. Es schließen sich ihr entlang der Fußgängerzone die Pfarrwohnung und der Kindergarten an. Die beruhigende Wirkung der Raumwand entsteht durch das Fassadenmaterial, ein hellgrauer, sorgfältig verarbeiteter Betonvorsatzstein, und die wenigen Öffnungen. Das Gebäude beherrscht den gegenüberliegenden Marktplatz nicht durch Masse, sondern durch seine schlanke Form und das schlichte Material.

Uhl entzog sich bei diesem wie bei all seinen anderen Bauten vorsätzlich jedem Ästhetizismus. Sein Anliegen ist es, die Gläubigen in den Mittelpunkt seiner architektonischen Überlegungen zu stellen und ihnen die interne Kommunikation auf einer demokratischen Basis zu ermöglichen.

Bei der Schlüsselübergabe der Kirche formulierte Uhl seine „Kirchenträume": *„Ich habe mir vorgestellt, dass dieses Haus ein Ort der Idee, der Diskussion, der offenen ungezwungenen Kritik auch an der Kirche sein könnte."*

Detail of the Gallery

Northern façade section

Northern façade of the community center

Interior church view

Interior church view featuring the glass block gallery and windbreaking structure

1983–1991
Museum of Modern Art
Frankfurt / Main, Germany
Hans Hollein

The Magistrate of the City Frankfurt founded the Museum of Modern Art in 1981 and announced an architectural competition for the building in 1982. Hans Hollein won the competition in 1983 and construction began in 1987.

Hans Hollein designed the unconventional Frankfurt Museum of Modern Art building over a triangular site plan, which is why Frankfurt locals call the building, "the piece of cake." Hollein chose this approach to facilitate the exhibition of modern art. The almost forty rooms meet requirements for installations, work groups and the presentation of paintings.

What helped the building earn worldwide recognition was the balanced interplay of architectural and artistic compositions. Hollein developed the building and the room sequence on the basis of the sites' architecturally unusual triangular shape and its symmetry. He also succeeded in making a walk through the museum a special experience with the sequence of connections, transitions, the views between the exhibition rooms, and the relation between the individual rooms as well as the ideal lighting.

The unconventional building geometry, the structuring of the façade with convex and concave surfaces that are partially interrupted by windows, the differing upper lighting structure and the interior organization, as well as the unusual ceiling heights posed challenges for the contractors, construction workers and all other participants.

Der Magistrat der Stadt Frankfurt gründete das Museum für Moderne Kunst 1981 und schrieb 1982 einen Architekturwettbewerb für das Gebäude aus, der 1983 von Hans Hollein gewonnen wurde. Baubeginn war im Juni 1987.

Das unkonventionelle Gebäude des Museums Moderner Kunst in Frankfurt über dreieckigem Grundriss – deshalb von den Frankfurtern „Tortenstück" genannt – wurde von Hans Hollein für Ausstellungen zeitgenössischer Kunst entworfen. Die knapp vierzig Räume werden den Ansprüchen von Installationen, Werkgruppen und der Präsentation von Bildern gerecht.

Was dem Bau weltweite Anerkennung brachte, ist das ausbalancierte Ineinandergreifen architektonischer und künstlerischer Inszenierung. Hollein entwickelte den Baukörper und die Raumfolge aus der für Architektur ungewöhnlichen Dreiecksform des Grundstücks und ihrer Symmetrie. Es gelang ihm dabei durch die Folge von Verbindungen, Übergängen und Durchblicken zwischen den Ausstellungsräumen, das Verhältnis der einzelnen Räume zueinander sowie die optimale Lichtführung einen Gang durch das Museum zu einem besonderen Erlebnis zu gestalten.

Die unkonventionelle Gebäudegeometrie, die Strukturierung der Fassade durch konvexe und konkave Flächen, zum Teil durch Fenster durchbrochen, die differenzierte Oberlichtarchitektur, der durchgegliederte Innenraum sowie ungewöhnliche Geschoßhöhen stellten hohe Ansprüche an Können und Flexibilität von Bauleitung, Bauhandwerkern und alle anderen Beteiligten.

Corner view

Exterior view

Corner view

Hall

Exhibition hall

1986–1992
Art and Exhibition Hall
Bonn, Germany
Gustav Peichl

A number of artists had already discussed the possibility of building an Art Exhibition Hall in Bonn as early as 1949. But the architectural competition for an art and exhibition hall for the German Federal Republic was only announced in 1985. 35 participants in the competition for the neighboring Bonn Art Museum were invited to submit entries as well as five foreign architects. The jury awarded the first prize to Gustav Peichl's design in July 1986.

Gustav Peichl designed a major structure and communications center. The site plan was based on the idea of a flexible use concept. Behind the 96 meter long façades of the cubic structure lies a service area with offices, workshops, meeting rooms, a library and three exhibition galleries. The inner square is divided into a foyer, large hall, atrium hall and forum. The exhibition spaces provide a differentiated system of small, middle and large rooms that can be used in varying configurations. The three light towers symbolize the triad of the fine arts: architecture, painting and sculpture. They supply light for the exhibition areas. The greenery on the roof works as a fifth façade and is used as the sculpture garden, providing additional exhibition space.

The 16 steel columns made of darkly patinated metal along the façade facing Friedrich-Ebert-Allee emphasize the construction lines and stand for the 16 German Federal Country Provinces.

Bereits 1949 wurde von zahlreichen Künstlern über eine Kunsthalle in Bonn diskutiert. Aber erst 1985 kam es zur Auslobung eines Architektenwettbewerbs für die Kunst- und Ausstellungshalle der Bundesrepublik Deutschland. Eingeladen waren 35 Teilnehmer aus dem Wettbewerb für das benachbarte Kunstmuseum Bonn sowie fünf zugeladene Architekten aus dem Ausland. Im Juli 1986 zeichnete die Jury den Entwurf von Gustav Peichl mit dem 1. Preis aus.

Gustav Peichl entwarf ein signifikantes Bauwerk und Kommunikationszentrum. Der Grundriß beruht auf der Idee eines flexiblen Nutzungskonzepts. Hinter den jeweils 96 Meter langen Fassaden des kubischen Baukörpers liegt eine Servicezone mit Büros, Werkstätten, Versammlungsräumen, Bibliothek und drei Ausstellungsgalerien. Das innere Quadrat teilt sich in Foyer, Große Halle, Atrium-Halle und Forum auf. Der Ausstellungsraum bietet ein differenziertes System von kleinen, mittleren und großen Räumen, das variabel genutzt werden kann. Die drei Lichttürme symbolisieren den Dreiklang der bildenden Künste – Architektur, Malerei und Skulptur. Sie sorgen für die Beleuchtung der Ausstellungsbereiche. Die bepflanzte Dachlandschaft als fünfte Fassade des Hauses wird als Skulpturengarten genutzt und erweitert somit die Ausstellungsfläche.

Die 16 Stahlsäulen aus dunkel patiniertem Metall entlang der Fassade an der Friedrich-Ebert-Allee betonen die Verbauungslinie und symbolisieren die deutschen Bundesländer.

First sketch for the competition

Northern façade with steel supports, the symbols of the federal countries and the main entrance

Main entrance with a view of the forecourt

Forecourt with sinus-shaped façade, red maple "Helmut", information column and entrance

Foyer, entrance and a view of the forecourt

Exhibition hall with light tower ("Territorium artis" Exhibition)

1988–1993
Johann Wolfgang Goethe University Biology Center
Frankfurt/Main, Germany
Wilhelm Holzbauer

Goethe University in Frankfurt am Main was the first university in Germany to be paid for by German citizens. The four university centers are spread over the entire city. Wilhelm Holzbauer and Ernst Mayr's Biology Center is located on the Niederurseler Hang Hill, the site of the "Riedberg Campus."

The existing chemistry department structures had to be integrated in the overall concept for the new building.

The objective was to create a university complex that would offer a balanced composition of the functional requirements and also offer an atmosphere of individuality in an appropriate scale through its architectural quality and its spatial sequence.

A fundamental differentiation was achieved between the central facilities and the basic research and teaching units in the structural composition of the building. The former are located in a longitudinal wing on the western side of the existing building, which also houses the main access system in form of a glass walkway. The cafeteria, lecture halls, library and overall university functions follow along this axle from the entrance.

Bridge-like structures establish a connection to the lab areas and the existing chemistry department buildings. The character of the landscape surrounding the complex should remain unchanged and be used in this form.

Die Goethe-Universität in Frankfurt am Main war die erste von Bürgern gestiftete Universität Deutschlands. Die vier Zentren der Universität sind über das gesamte Stadtgebiet verteilt. Der Niederurseler Hang, wo sich der „Campus Riedberg" befindet, ist der Standort des Biozentrums von Wilhelm Holzbauer und Ernst Mayr.

Bei der Planung mussten die bestehenden Bauten des Fachbereiches Chemie in das Gesamtkonzept integriert werden.

Es sollte ein Universitätskomplex geschaffen werden, der in seiner architektonischen Haltung und in seiner räumlichen Gliederung eine ausgewogene Komposition zwischen den funktionellen Erfordernissen darstellt und zugleich eine Atmosphäre von Individualität und Maßstäblichkeit erzeugt.

In der baulichen Komposition ist eine deutliche Unterscheidung zwischen den zentralen Einrichtungen einerseits und den Grundeinheiten für Forschung und Lehre andererseits getroffen. Erstere sind in einem an der Westseite der bestehenden Gebäude angeordneten Längstrakt situiert, der auch das zentrale Aufschließungssystem in Form einer gläsernen Passage beinhaltet. Ausgehend vom Eingangsbereich sind an dieser Achse die Mensa, Hörsäle, Bibliothek und gesamtuniversitäre Funktionen untergebracht.

Brückenartige Bauwerke stellen die Verbindung zu den Laborbereichen sowie zum bestehenden Chemiegebäude her. Der den baulichen Komplex umgebende Landschaftsraum soll in seinem Charakter unverändert belassen und in dieser Gestalt genutzt werden.

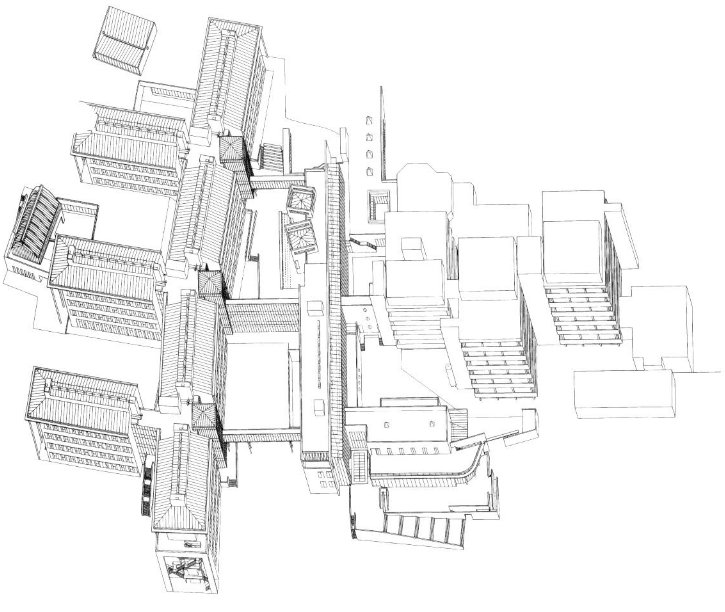

Axonometry

Lecture hall

Façade

Staircase spindle

1991–1997
Landeszentralbank Potsdam
Berlin, Germany
Ortner & Ortner

Ortner & Ortner describe the location of the Landeszentralbank in Potsdam: *"'Suburban Berlin' is the name of the villa area to the northeast of the center of Potsdam. The new Landeszentralbank building will be part of the park area, without claiming special status. It consists of two independent buildings: three town houses that are linked by a common terrace course that will compose the actual bank building across the way from the Kleist villa."*

The new building blends smoothly with the existing surroundings. This consists of townhouses in which the bank's staff and director live, the earlier building and the generous park along Berliner Straße. On the outside, the three-level bank building appears to be rectangular box whose length along the sides takes up the depth of the site. Three sides of the building are clad with natural stone and only sparingly opened. The block features a projecting, glass-clad entrance hall along the entire length of the front. Ortner & Ortner have a reason for calling this hall the "showcase." From the outside, one can recognize two elevator towers, a stairway and two bridges surrounded by a "golden cage," which provides access from the elevators to the customer service areas. At the core of the building lies a 540 square-meter safe that is surrounded by safety measures that were elegantly paneled by the architects.

Ortner & Ortner beschreiben die Lage der Landeszentralbank in Potsdam: *„'Berliner Vorstadt' heißt die Villengegend nordöstlich des Potsdamer Zentrums. Der Neubau der Landeszentralbank fügt sich in das Parkareal, ohne bevorzugten Status für sich zu reklamieren. Er setzt sich aus zwei selbständigen Gebäuden zusammen: Drei Stadtvillen, die durch einen gemeinsamen Terrassensockel zusammengefaßt das Vis-à-Vis der Kleist'schen Villa und das eigentliche Bankgebäude bilden."*

Der Neubau fügt sich geschickt in das bestehende Ambiente ein. Dieses besteht aus den von Mitarbeitern und vom Direktor der Bank bewohnten Stadtvillen sowie der früheren Dienststelle und dem großzügigen, an der Berliner Straße gelegenen Park. Nach außen hin tritt das drei Stock hohe Bankgebäude als rechteckige Kiste auf, deren Längsseiten sich in die Tiefe des Grundstücks erstrecken. Drei Seiten des Gebäudes sind mit Naturstein verkleidet und nur spärlich geöffnet. Straßenseitig ist dem Block eine seine gesamte Höhe und Breite einnehmende verglaste Eingangshalle vorgelagert. Ortner & Ortner nennen diese Halle nicht von ungefähr „Vitrine". Man erkennt von außen zwei Fahrstuhltürme, eine Treppenanlage und zwei von einem „goldenen Käfig" umschlossene Brücken, über die man vom Fahrstuhl in die Kundenbereiche der Bank gelangt. Kern des Gebäudes ist ein 540 Quadratmeter großer Tresor, der von Sicherheitsvorkehrungen, die architektonisch elegant verkleidet sind, umgeben ist.

Complete Project, birds' eye view

Bank building and the three town houses

Glass façade/Stone facade

Metal steps

Detail of the metal mesh cladding used on the staircase

1993
Experimental Residential Project, IGA (International Gardening Exhibition) Stuttgart, Germany Szyszkowitz - Kowalski

In 1993, the City of Stuttgart hosted an international gardening fair. The theme was "Living 2000." The City fathers saw a unique opportunity to complement the concepts begun in previous Federal Gardening Fairs with a large city park landscape. The green belt around Stuttgart was to be completed as part of the fair. This intention included plans for new inner-city housing projects to be realized within these green areas. The guiding theme of these experimental projects was, "responsible living with nature and the city." The invited architects made planning suggestions in keeping with today's technologies, which make ecologically sound architecture possible (earth-protected, passive/solar and energy-saving construction techniques). At the same time, measures were to be taken against unfavorable influences on urban living (rail and car traffic, etc.).

Szyszkowitz - Kowalski created a building with a low-slung, vaulted roof using an expressive language of forms that is derived from the structure's energy concept. The building became the most salient structure in the group of houses. The interior distribution was designed in accordance with the heating requirements. The living area faces south while the bedrooms; kitchen and bathrooms are aligned to the north. Hence the south side is transparent and light, while the north side is massive and closed.

Die Stadt Stuttgart veranstaltete 1993 die Internationale Gartenbauausstellung mit dem Thema „Wohnen 2000". Die Stadtväter sahen darin die einmalige Chance, die mit vorangegangenen Bundesgartenschauen begonnenen Konzepte einer großzügigen Stadtparklandschaft zu vollenden. Im Zuge dieser Ausstellung sollte der Grüngürtel rund um Stuttgart geschlossen werden, wobei entsprechend der stadtplanerischen Zielsetzung auch innerhalb dieser Naturräume neue innerstädtische Wohnanlagen realisiert werden sollten. Das Leitthema für diesen experimentellen Wohnungsbau lautete „verantwortungsbewusster Umgang mit Natur und Stadt". Die eingeladenen Architekten hatten Planungsvorschläge hinsichtlich der heute möglichen Techniken des naturschonenden Bauens (erdgeschützte, passiv-solare und energiesparende Bauweise usw.) zu entwickeln. Zugleich sollten Vorkehrungen gegen die im städtischen Bereich bestehenden ungünstigen Einflüsse (Schienen- und Straßenverkehr usw.) getroffen werden.

Szyszkowitz - Kowalski schufen einen Bau, der durch sein tiefgezogenes Tonnendach und seine expressive Formensprache, die sich aus dem Energiekonzept herleitete, zur auffallendsten Hausgruppe der Siedlung wurde. Die Aufteilung im Inneren richtet sich nach dem Wärmebedarf. Wohnräume sind nach Süden, Schlafräume, Küche und Bäder nach Norden orientiert. Dem entspricht, dass sich die Südseite transparent und leicht, die Nordseite dagegen massiv und geschlossen darstellt.

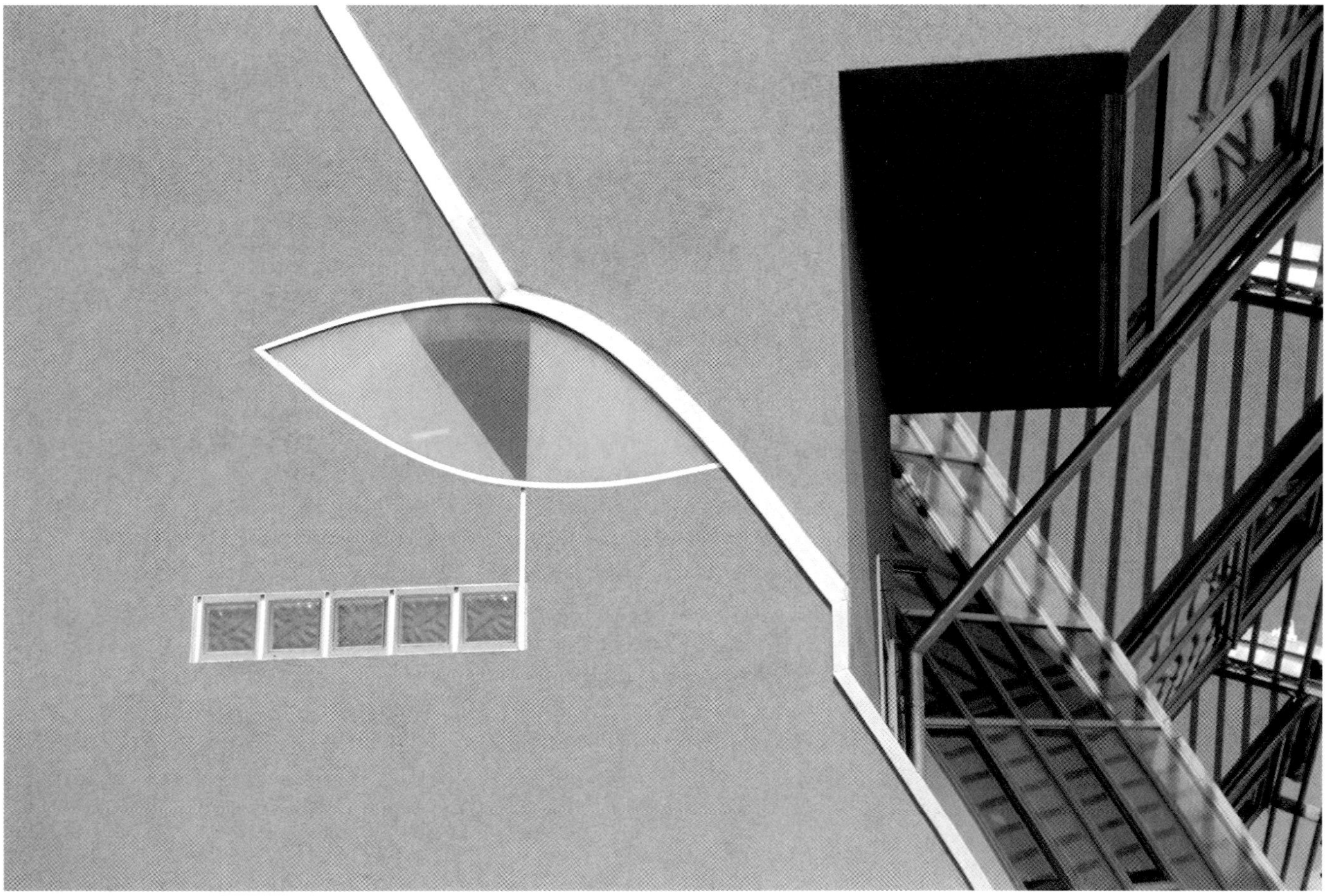

Detail of the lateral façade

Few of the complete project

Detail of the front façade

1993–1995
Groninger Museum, East Pavilion
Groningen, The Netherlands
Coop Himmelb(l)au

In 1988, the Milanese architect and designer Alessandro Mendini was commissioned to redesign the Museum of the City of Groningen. Mendini designed the entrance area himself, but he hired internationally recognized architects such as Michele de Lucchi, Philippe Starck and Coop Himmelb(l)au to design the individual museum sections and the East pavilion for visiting exhibitions.

The museum is an Island that represents the link between the train station and the city. Some of the museum's pavilions are even partly blow the water surface. The East pavilion, however, hovers above the water. The architects were inspired by shipbuilding for their design. Its deconstructed form consists of large, double-faced steel panels that are linked to one another with tempered glass panels in the absence of metal joints. The walls were made exclusively of steel and glass to allow daylight to stream in on unusual spots.

The architect's objective was to create interplay between the outside and inside and surprise the visitor with unexpected views. Walking routes on different levels – including an overhead walkway that intersects all the rooms – make it possible to view the works of art from different perspectives.

1988 wurde der Mailänder Architekt und Designer Alessandro Mendini beauftragt, das Museum der Stadt Groningen neu zu gestalten. Mendini entwarf den Eingangsbereich selbst. Für die einzelnen, als Gebäude in sich abgeschlossenen Abteilungen aber beauftragte er international bekannte Baukünstler wie Michele de Lucchi, Philippe Starck und Coop Himmelb(l)au, die den Ostpavillon für die Wechselausstellungen des Museums gestalteten.

Das Museum ist eine Insel, welche die Verbindung zwischen der Bahnstation und der Stadt darstellt. Einige Pavillons des Museums befinden sich sogar teilweise unter dem Wasserspiegel. Der Ostpavillon hingegen schwebt gleichsam über dem Wasser. Bei seiner Konstruktion ließen sich die Architekten von der Schiffsbauweise inspirieren. Seine dekonstruktivistische Form setzt sich aus großen doppelwandigen Stahlplatten zusammen, die dort, wo sie nicht direkt aneinander schließen, mit gehärteten Glasscheiben verbunden werden. Die Wände wurden ausschließlich aus Stahl und Glas konstruiert, um auch an ungewöhnlichen Stellen den Einfall von Tageslicht zu ermöglichen.

Ziel der Architekten war es, eine Wechselwirkung zwischen innen und außen zu erreichen, um den Besucher mit unerwarteten Ausblickmöglichkeiten zu überraschen. Wandelrouten auf verschiedenen Ebenen – darunter eine Laufbrücke, die quer durch die Räume führt – ermöglichen es, die Kunstwerke von unterschiedlichen Blickwinkeln zu betrachten.

Exterior view

View of the interior

Stairs leading to the outside

Exhibition room

Exhibition room

1993–1998
UFA Cinema Palace
Dresden, Germany
Coop Himmelb(l)au

The UFA Cinema Palace close to the main train station in Dresden is Germany's second largest cinema complex. Coop Himmelb(l)au expanded the existing round cinema by adding eight theaters that can seat 2.600 moviegoers. The deconstructive structure offers a stark contrast to the prefabricated slab buildings stemming from the GDR era.

The crystalline structure of the building that caused UFA to call it the "Crystal Palace," was made possible by using a steel skeleton support system for the glass-clad surfaces. Staircases and walkways set at an angle offer access to the individual theaters in the central circular cement structure from the entrance and foyer area. During the day, sunlight is broken by the daringly angled glass surfaces, allowing for an unimpeded view of the inside. At night, the palace is lit with changing lights, which also submerge the surrounding prefabricated buildings in lights of different colors.

The foyer that this building is actually about is neither an inside nor an outside space. Coop Himmelb(l)au on the subject: *"The Skybar, the 'floating' double-cone inside the foyer, is accessible and will host different functions (café, bar etc.). In this way, the content of the building becomes visible to the city as much as the city is visible from the building. It is an inside-out building, which sustains a dialogue with the city. The media event – projected from the interior towards the exterior – assists in the creation of urban space."*

Der UFA Kinopalast in der Nähe des Hauptbahnhofes in Dresden ist das zweitgrößte Kino Deutschlands. Coop Himmelb(l)au erweiterten das bestehende Rundkino um acht Säle mit rund 2.600 Sitzplätzen. Die dekonstruktivistische Konstruktion steht im krassen Gegensatz zu den sie umgebenden Plattenbauten der DDR-Zeit.

Die kristalline Struktur des Bauwerks, die ihm den von der UFA propagierten Beinamen „Kristallpalast" eintrug, wird durch die von einer Stahlskelett-Konstruktion getragenen Glasflächen bewirkt. Der Eingangs- und Foyerbereich erschließt über verwinkelt verlaufende Treppen und Stege die einzelnen Kinosäle in dem mittig gelegenen Betonrundbau mit den Kinosälen. Tagsüber wird das Sonnenlicht in den kühn geneigten Glasflächen gebrochen und gibt den Blick in das Innere frei. Nachts wird der Palast von wechselnden Leuchten erhellt, die auch die umgebenden Plattenbauten in verschiedenfarbiges Licht tauchen.

Das Foyer, um das es bei dem Bau eigentlich geht, ist weder Innen- noch Außenraum. Coop Himmelb(l)au schreiben darüber: *"The Skybar, the 'floating' double-cone inside the foyer, is accessible and will host different functions (café, bar etc.). In this way, the content of the building becomes visible to the city as much as the city is visible from the building. It is an inside-out building which sustains a dialogue with the city. The media event – projected from the interior towards the exterior – assists in the creation of urban space."*

Exterior view

Exterior view

Interior with seating

Interior with stairway access

Interior, view of the elevator tower

1993–1999
Haus am Zwinger
Dresden, Germany
Heinz Tesar

Heinz Tesar's buildings are influenced by examples from antiquity and the Renaissance in terms of their proportions and scale, although he cannot be considered a traditionalist. However, Tesar's buildings are in keeping with the traditions of specific Viennese Modernists, the most famous of which were Adolf Loos and Josef Frank. The fronts of his buildings with their stringently perforated façades and few windows appear to be studies in weight, while the interiors are light and airy. Tesar makes careful use of material and color contrasts.

Tesar designed three projects for Dresden: the synagogue, a museum concept and the Haus am Zwinger. Of these proposals, only the Haus am Zwinger was realized. Tesar won the competition for an office building on the southern side of the Palais Taschenberg, today's Hotel Kempinski in 1993. In the Haus am Zwinger, Tesar blended Renaissance and Baroque elements to create a unique composition. The 170 meter long, 15 meter deep and 18.5 meter building is at a distance to the surrounding buildings. But three walkways that intersect the building keep it from becoming a hermetic block between the palace and the surrounding structures. A hook that swings out towards the southern pavilion of the cage provides the head of the building. Conic pilasters at five-meter intervals made of steel featuring cornices support the façades. A zone with two-level office units follows on top, which insinuate a Renaissance-like conclusion of the building's upper section.

Hinsichtlich Proportionen und Maßstab sind Tesars Bauten von Vorbildern aus Antike und Renaissance geprägt, obwohl er keineswegs traditionell baut. Tesars Bauten stehen aber auch in der Tradition der spezifischen Wiener Moderne, deren bekannteste Vertreter Adolf Loos und Josef Frank sind. Die Fronten seiner Gebäude mit strengen Lochfassaden und meist wenigen Fenstern erscheinen als Etüden auf die Schwere, während das Innere hell und luftig ist. Material- und Farbkontrast setzt Tesar behutsam ein.

Für Dresden entwarf Tesar drei Projekte: die Synagoge, ein Museumskonzept und das Haus am Zwinger. Verwirklicht davon wurde das Haus am Zwinger. Tesar hatte 1993 bei einem Wettbewerb den Sieg für das Bürohaus an der Südseite des Palais Taschenberg, dem heutigen Hotel Kempinski, errungen. Renaissance und Barock vermengte Tesar beim Haus am Zwinger zu einer eigenwilligen Komposition. Der 170 Meter lange, 15 Meter tiefe und 18,5 Meter hohe Baukörper bewahrt Abstand gegenüber den umliegenden Bauten. Drei Durchgänge im Haus verhindern jedoch, dass es zu einem hermetischen Riegel zwischen Palais und die umgebenden Wohnbauten wird. Der Kopf des Baukörpers bildet einen Haken, der gegenüber dem Südpavillon des Zwingers ausschwingt. Im 5-Meter-Abstand gliedern konische Pilaster aus Stahl, die ein Gesims tragen, die Fassaden. Darüber folgt eine Zone mit zweigeschossigen Büroeinheiten, die eine renaissancehafte Auflösung des Baukörpers nach oben hin ankündigen.

Gable end with the cage in the background

Façade segment

Gable end, façade section with walkways

Vestibule on the upper level

Hall

1994–1995
Holz-Altenried Company Building
Hergatz, Germany
Baumschlager & Eberle

The bold, three-dimensional shape of the building and its larch timber cladding, which creates a seamless transition to the roof, make it clear that this company's substance is selling and working with wood without any additional signs. The broad showcase front that faces the road in front of it is an eye catcher. In accordance with this, the front section of the building houses the exhibition and sales area that can be reached from the roadside. Seven large garage doors lead to the warehouse area. The walls and the ceiling below the exhibition area in this section are finished with cement. Everything else is made of timber. The exhibition room is dominated by the bonded fir timber construction method. The monolithic design of the building reminds visitors of shipbuilding. Slit-like windows were cut into the stern of this ship, behind which lie the offices and social areas. The orange-colored narrow end of the building was designed with future expansion possibilities in mind.

The building is in keeping with Baumschlager & Eberle's guiding principles since it is a blend of traditional and modern technologies.

Die markante plastische Gestalt des Gebäudes und seine Lärchenholzverkleidung, die fugenlos in das Dach übergeht, signalisieren ohne weitere Aufschrift, dass es sich um einen Betrieb handelt, der Holz verarbeitet und vertreibt. Eine breite Schaufensterfront, die zur naheliegenden Bundesstraße gerichtet ist, ist als Blickfang angelegt. Der vordere Teil des Gebäudes beherbergt demgemäss den von der Straßenseite aus zugänglichen Ausstellungs- und Verkaufsbereich. An der Rückseite führen sieben große Garagentore zum Lagerbereich. Hier sind die Außenwände und die Zwischendecke zum Ausstellungsbereich betoniert. Alles andere ist aus Holz. Der Ausstellungsraum wird von der mächtigen Leimbinderkonstruktion aus Fichtenholz beherrscht. Die monolithische Gestalt des Gebäudes weckt Erinnerungen an den Schiffsbau. Im Bug dieses Schiffes sind über Eck schlitzartige Fenster eingeschnitten, hinter denen sich die Büros und Sozialräume befinden. Die orange gestrichene Schmalseite am Ende des Einraum-Ausstellungsbereichs wurde für künftige Erweiterungs- und Anbaumöglichkeiten ausgelegt.

Indem das Gebäude traditionelle und moderne technologische Baumethoden vereinigt, wird es den Grundsätzen der Architektur von Baumschlager & Eberle gerecht.

Front side with showcase windows

Exhibition and sales room

Rear side with garage doors

1994–1996
Küppersbuschgelände Residential Project, IBA (Internationale Bauausstellung) Gelsenkirchen, Germany Szyszkowitz - Kowalski

There is a certain irony in the fact that a 350 square kilometer natural park is named after a strip of brackish sewage water, the Emscher River, which flows over 70 kilometers through the Ruhr in Germany via a canalization system. The theme of the exhibition was the renewal of a run-down industrial region. During the IBA, landmark buildings of the industrial era were given new functions and transformed into jewels of the age of industrialization, while abandoned spaces were linked together to create one cohesive park landscape. The result of the building exhibition was proof that *Gartenstadtsiedlung* (Garden City Housing Project) is a suitable solution for re-gentrification projects. It also proved that unusual and inspired solutions offered at reasonable prices can lead to housing that is as good as it is anywhere else.

In 1999, the Küppersbuschgelände Housing Project built by Szyszkowitz - Kowalski won the German Architecture Prize. The reasons stated by the jury were, amongst others: *"Although it was planned and completed in one continuous process, this project seems to have grown like a village. Many things are reminiscent of a village: the open space at the center, the small scale of the houses and the blend of tenants. A central IBA credo – the careful handling of rain water – was clearly addressed with the surrounding, high-walled rain gutter, which also accentuates the contours of the public spaces."*

Es ist nicht ohne Ironie, dass ein brackiger Abwasserstreifen, die Emscher, die komplett kanalisiert über siebzig Kilometer Länge durch das nördliche Ruhrgebiet fließt, das für den 350 Quadratkilometer großen Landschaftspark namensgebende Rückrat bildet. Thema der Bauausstellung war die Erneuerung einer in weiten Teilen brachgefallenen Industrieregion. Im Rahmen der IBA erhielten Baudenkmale des Industriezeitalters im Ruhrgebiet neue Funktionen, wurden zu Pretiosen der Industriegeschichte verwandelt, und brachliegende Areale wurden zu einer zusammenhängenden Parklandschaft verknüpft. Ein Ergebnis der Bauausstellung ist, dass die Gartenstadtsiedlung dafür geeignet ist, das Problem zu lösen, Menschen auf ebenso ungewöhnliche wie inspirierende Weise zu mäßigen Preisen so gut wie nur irgend möglich zu behausen.

1999 wurde die Wohnsiedlung Küppersbuschgelände von Szyszkowitz - Kowalski mit dem Deutschen Architekturpreis ausgezeichnet. In der Begründung der Jury heißt es unter anderem: *„Obwohl in einem Zug geplant und realisiert, wirkt diese Wohnanlage gewachsen wie ein Dorf. Auch vieles andere erinnert an ein Dorf: der Anger im Zentrum, die Kleinmaßstäblichkeit der Häuser, die Mischung der Bewohnerschaft. Ein zentrales Credo der IBA – der sorgsame Umgang mit dem Regenwasser – wird in Form einer umlaufenden, aufgeständerten Rinne deutlich sichtbar inszeniert, wodurch zugleich die Konturen des öffentlichen Raums verdeutlicht werden."*

Airside view

Courtyard in the center of the project with raised rain gutters

Courtyard in the center of the project

Supported rain gutter

Residential project segment

1994–2002
Vulcania, European Vulcanism Center
Clermont-Ferrand, France
Hans Hollein

Valéry Giscard d´Estaing, the former French President and current regional president of Auvergne presided over the opening of the "Vulcania" Museum close to Clermont-Ferrand in February 2002, after eight years of construction. Among the population, the project is known as the "Giscardoscope." The "Vulcania" Museum is a museum of natural history that concentrates on vulcanism. Hollein built three quarters of the premises – the exhibition surfaces cover a total of 4,700 meters – on the site of an ammunition depot that is located on a plateau 1,000 meters above sea level.

The landmark of the "Parc européen du volcanisme" which covers a total of 57 hectares is a 28 meter-high cone that symbolically represents the cross-section of a volcano. On the insides, light streams in over the gold-colored titanium panels, leading the way in. The visitor, who is supposed to be taken on a "research journey to the depths of the earth," should experience this "entrance" via the unusual architecture. The museum spaces are aligned in a radial sequence around the cone. These include two cinemas and dense, compact information on Volcanoes and volcanic research as well as general geological history and the history of the Auvergne region in particular.

Die Eröffnung des nach achtjähriger Bauzeit fertiggestellten „Vulcania"-Museums in der Nähe von Clermont-Ferrand wurde im Februar 2002 vom ehemaligen französischen Staatspräsidenten und nunmehrigen Regionalpräsidenten der Auvergne, Valéry Giscard d´Estaing, vorgenommen. Nach ihm wird das Projekt im Volksmund auch „Giscardoscope" genannt. Das „Vulcania" ist ein naturkundliches Museum, das sich auf Vulkanismus konzentriert. Drei Viertel der Kubatur – die Ausstellungsfläche beträgt insgesamt 4.700 Quadratmeter – baute Hollein kilometerweit von jeglicher Zivilisation entfernt in ein ehemaliges Munitionsdepot ein, das sich auf einem rund 1.000 Meter Seehöhe gelegenen Hochplateau befindet.

Das Wahrzeichen des „Parc européen du volcanisme", der insgesamt 57 Hektar umfasst, ist ein 28 Meter hoher Konus, der symbolisch einen aufgeschnittenen Vulkankegel darstellt. An seinen Innenseiten wird das Licht über goldfarbene Titanplatten in das Innere geleitet. Dem Besucher, der hier zu einem „Forschungsreisenden ins Innere der Erde" wird, soll durch die außergewöhnliche Architektur das Erlebnis des „Eindringens in die Erde" vermittelt werden. Es erwarten ihn in den radial um den Konus angeordneten Museumsräumlichkeiten zwei Kinosäle und dichte, kompakte Informationen über Vulkane und ihre Erforschung sowie über die Erdgeschichte im Allgemeinen und die Auvergne im Besonderen.

Looking through the cone

The site as seen from the crater

Aerial view of the vulcane cone, crater and vulcanic garden

Crater

Vulcanic garden

1995–1998
Festival House
Baden-Baden, Germany
Wilhelm Holzbauer

The idea of a festival house for the spa and resort town of Baden-Baden was conceived in 1994, when it was suggested that the Salzburg Whitsun Festival be moved to Baden-Baden. After a so-called "American Process," i.e. interviewing the architects before making a selection, Wilhelm Holzbauer was commissioned to complete the project. The site provided by the city lies right behind the neo-classical train station that was closed down in 1977. Staggered into three levels, the block of the festival house rises above the entire breadth of the back of the train station to a height of 33 meters. Ivy-dressed obelisks with golden tips are the only elements that delineate the façade. Above looms the turquoise stage tower. The 700 square meter hall can accommodate up 2,650 guests. This large number is possible due to the two balconies and the five lateral levels. By using separating panels, the audience space can be sectioned off to provide 1,800, 1,300 or 1,000 seats.

In order to create an intimate atmosphere despite the size of the hall, the cement walls were finished with red stucco. A chandelier consisting of 10,000 hand-cut prisms, which also serves to hold the reflectors, was also mounted. A shell-shaped roof over the entire hall provides outstanding acoustics. The stage size can be adjusted via movable portals, while the orchestra pit can be raised to the seating level.

Die Idee eines Festspielhauses in der Kur- und Spielstadt Baden-Baden entstand 1994 aus der Überlegung, die Salzburger Pfingstfestspiele nach Baden-Baden zu verlegen. Nach einem sogenannten „amerikanischen Verfahren", einem Interview zur Wahl des Architekten, wurde Wilhelm Holzbauer mit der Ausführung beauftragt. Das von der Stadt zur Verfügung gestellte Grundstück liegt direkt hinter dem 1977 stillgelegten neoklassizistischen Bahnhof. Dreifach gestuft, steigt über die gesamte Breite der Rückfront des Bahnhofes der Block des Festspielhauses auf eine Höhe von 33 Meter. Efeuberankte Obelisken mit goldenen Spitzen bilden die einzige Gliederung der Fassade. Darüber ragt der türkisblaue Bühnenturm auf. Der 700 Quadratmeter große Saal des Festspielhauses kann bis zu 2.650 Hörer aufnehmen. Diese große Zahl an Zuhörern ist durch die zwei Balkone und fünf Seitenränge möglich. Mit Hilfe von Trennwänden kann der Zuschauerraum innerhalb von zehn Minuten auf 1.800, 1.300 oder 1.000 Plätze verkleinert werden.

Um trotz der Größe des Saales eine intime Atmosphäre zu schaffen, sind die Betonwände mit rotem Stucco antico gespachtelt und ein Luster aus 10.000 handgeschliffenen Kristallprismen, der gleichzeitig Lichtträger für Reflektoren ist, angebracht. Eine Dachschale über dem rechteckigen Saal sorgt für hervorragende Akustik. Die Bühne ist durch drei seitlich fahrbare Portale variabel. Der Orchestergraben kann auf die Höhe des Parketts hochgefahren werden.

Exterior view with the closed train station in front

Foyer on the lower level

Foyer on the upper level

View of the stage from the auditorium

View of the auditorium to the stage

1995–1999
ARD Capital City Television Studios
Berlin, Germany
Ortner & Ortner

Ortner & Ortner built the ARD Capital City Studios in Berlin, as well as an office and commercial building on Pariser Platz Square, a photonics center in Adlershof and the Landeszentralbank in Potsdam.

The perforated façade made of terracotta-red unfinished cement with flush-mounted exterior glass paneling of the main ARD studio snuggles up to the edge of Spree River shore next to the Reichstag with artistic verve. Thus it fits in alongside the surrounding the technical and natural sciences of Berlin University. The façade features protruding wooden windows in front of the "actual" façade. The breaks in the front create a fine graphical pattern and also make the change of function between the television and radio areas visible on the outside. A somewhat smaller connecting building complies with the Berlin building code that requires 20 per cent of a buildings' volume to be dedicated to residential space.

Ortner & Ortner explained their planning intentions as follows: ***"As part of one of the country's leading media companies, the ARD Capital City Studio occupies a central position along the Spree, across the street from the Reichstag, so to speak. The structure has character, as does the institution: it is firm and confident, earnest without being pathetic. It stabilizes its historical urban surroundings without conveying a superficial sense of media presence on the outside. Only the large window over the Wilhelmstrasse entrance indicates its function."***

Neben den ARD-Hauptstadtstudios errichteten Ortner & Ortner in Berlin ein Büro- und Geschäftshaus am Pariser Platz, ein Photonikzentrum in Adlershof und die Landeszentralbank in Potsdam.

Die Lochfassade aus terrakottarotem Sichtbeton mit außenbündiger Fixverglasung des ARD-Hauptstadtstudios schmiegt sich mit malerischem Schwung an das Reichstagufer der Spree und passt sich in das Ensemble der umgebenden technisch-naturwissenschaftlichen Institute der Berliner Universität ein. Die Fassade ist der „eigentlichen" Fassade mit Holzfenstern vorgestellt. Das Fugenspiel der Fronten zeichnet einerseits ein feines graphisches Muster und macht andererseits den Funktionswechsel vom Radio- zum Fernsehbereich außen erkennbar. In einem etwas niedrigeren anschließenden Gebäude wird dem Berliner Gesetz, dass 20 Prozent des Volumens Wohnungen vorbehalten sein müssen, genüge getan.

Ortner & Ortner erläutern ihre Intentionen bei der Planung: *„Als eine der führenden Medienanstalten des Landes bezieht das ARD-Hauptstadtstudio seine Position in zentraler Lage an der Spree, dem Reichstag sozusagen vis-a-vis. Der Bau hat wie die Institution Charakter: fest und selbstbewusst, mit unpathetischer Ernsthaftigkeit. Stabilisierend im Stadtgefüge ergänzt er den historischen Baublock ohne vordergründige Medialität im äußeren Erscheinungsbild. Lediglich das 'große Fenster' über dem Eingang in der Wilhelmstraße verweist auf die Funktion."*

Front façade detail

View of the complete project

Access walkway

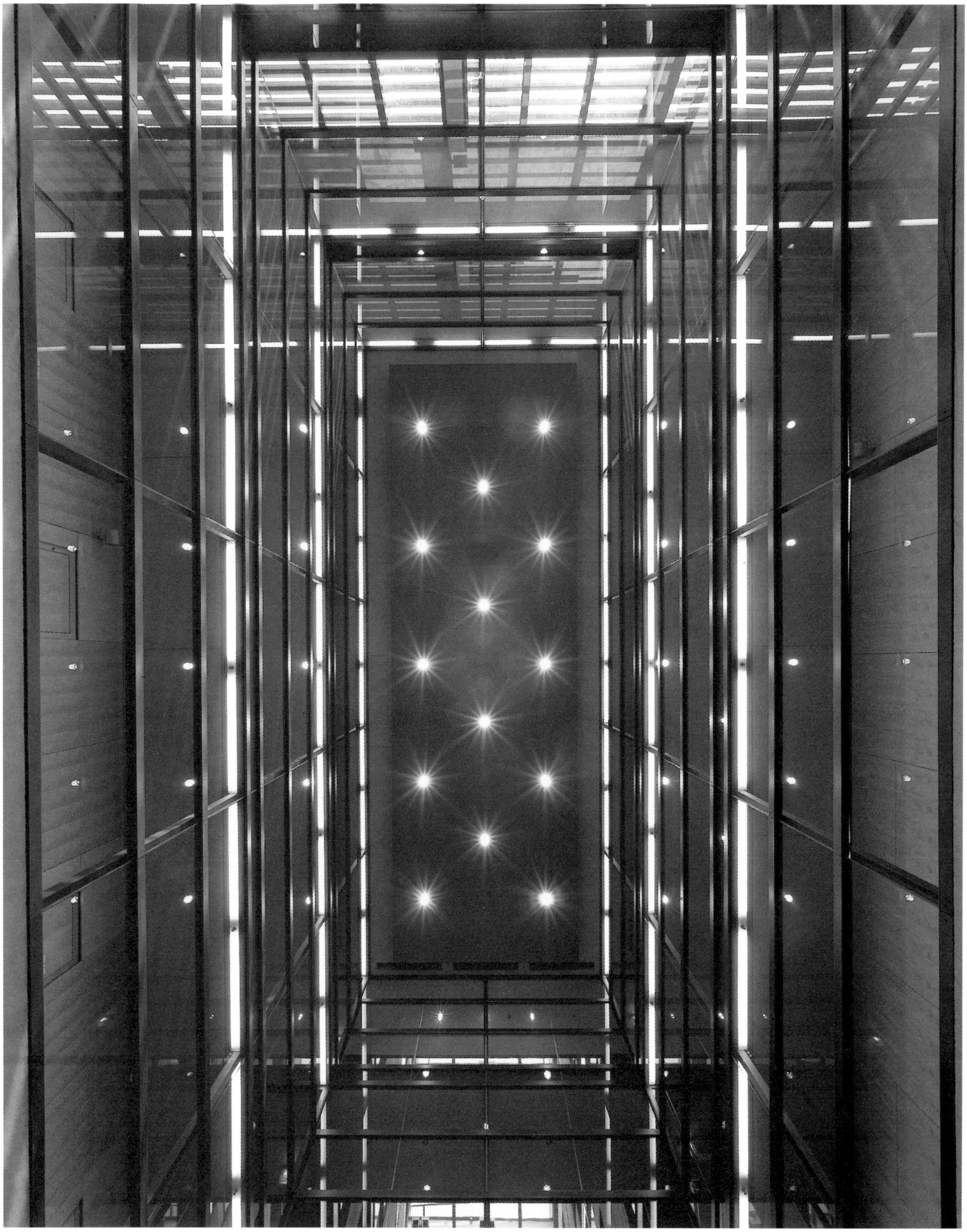

View of the Ceiling

Entrance area (Stairway)

1995–1999
Embassies of the Nordic Countries
Berlin, Germany
Berger + Parkkinen

The first phase of the competition to build the embassies of the Nordic countries (Denmark, Finland, Iceland, Norway and Sweden) was concluded in Berlin in December of 1995. Berger + Parkkinen, the Austrian-Finnish team of architects were awarded the first prize. Their proposed project was a building complex consisting of five embassy buildings, the meeting hall ("Felleshus") and a continuous lower level enclosed in a 226-meter long and 14.8-meter high copper ribbon. They were also entrusted with the urban construction coordination. Separate competitions took place for the individual embassy buildings in the second phase. However, the spatial parameters and the architectural concept were defined by the winning proposal in the first phase.

The "Felleshus" is the most frequented area of the complex since it also functions as the entrance. Embassy access is coordinated at the reception, which is also the site of the consular services counters. An auditorium (readings, concerts) is available for the guests, as well as exhibition spaces, conference and VIP facilities. There is also a restaurant that is open to both staff members and guests. A stripe-shaped timber façade gives the public areas unmistakably atmospheric light.

Each of the five countries was assigned its own "embassy cube." The small Nordic village is grouped around a common square, narrow alleys and bodies of water.

Im Dezember 1995 wurde die erste Phase des Wettbewerbs für die Botschaften der Nordischen Länder (Dänemark, Finnland, Island, Norwegen, Schweden) in Berlin entschieden. Den 1. Preis gewann das österreichisch-finnische Architektenteam Berger + Parkkinen, deren Projekt einen Gebäudekomplex vorsah, bestehend aus den fünf Botschaftsgebäuden, dem Gemeinschaftshaus („Felleshus") und einem durchgehenden Tiefgeschoß, umschlossen von einem 226 Meter langen und 14,8 Meter hohen Kupferband. Weiters wurden sie mit der städtebaulichen Koordination des Gesamtprojektes beauftragt. In der zweiten Phase fanden getrennte Wettbewerbe für die Entwürfe zu den einzelnen Botschaftsgebäuden statt, wobei das Siegerprojekt der ersten Phase die räumlichen Vorgaben und das architektonische Konzept bestimmte.

Das „Felleshus" ist als Eingangsgebäude der Anlage der am meisten besuchte Teil. In der Rezeption wird der Zugang zu den Botschaften geregelt. Auch die Schalter für die konsularischen Dienste befinden sich hier. Für das Publikum stehen ein Auditorium (Lesungen, Konzerte), Ausstellungsräume, Konferenz- und V. I. P.-Räume sowie ein Restaurant für Personal und Gäste zur Verfügung. Eine streifenförmige Holzfassade gibt den öffentlichen Bereichen eine unverwechselbare Lichtstimmung.

In der Anlage wurde jedem der fünf Länder ein eigener „Botschaftskubus" zugeteilt. Das kleine nordische Dorf gruppiert sich um einen gemeinsamen Platz, schmale Gassen und Wasserflächen.

Copper ribbon cladding connecting the six buildings of the Scandinavian embassies

Common building

Central glass-clad stairway in the reception area

Reception and lounge area of the common building

Consulate of the five Nordic Countries on the ground floor of the common building

1996
Glass Pavilion
Neuilly sur Seine, Paris, France
Dietmar Feichtinger

Structurally challenging designs are the trademark of "Feichtinger Architectes," which was founded by Dietmar Feichtinger in 1994. The glass pavilion covering a surface of 240 square meters for an international law and tax consultants firm lies within a courtyard and connects three office buildings. It serves as a reception and meeting place and is characterized by the extreme delicacy of its structure. The inner courtyard is designed to act as a garden. The completely transparent façades establish a link to the garden. The roof consists of a glass panel with a diameter of 14 meters. The glass is plated and the individual panels are supported at four points. The panel is suspended on steel cables. These provide stable support via their steel tension ring mounting. The steel ring lies on cross-shaped solid steel struts.

The structure of the pavilion consists of an elliptical double ring made of tubes that are located on the edges. Four cross-shaped struts support the ring. These struts create a pressure ring that provides tension for a double net of cables. Both cable constructions are connected with solid steel tension rods. The parabolic form of the first vertical net was achieved by using tension rods of varying lengths. They stiffen the glass roof and help absorb the loads that act on the glass surfaces.

Konstruktiv anspruchsvolle Entwürfe sind das Markenzeichen der jungen Firma „Feichtinger Architectes", die 1994 von Dietmar Feichtinger gegründet wurde. Der Glaspavillon über einer Baufläche von 240 Quadratmeter für eine internationale Rechtsanwalts- und Steuerberatungsgesellschaft liegt in einem Innenhof und verbindet drei Bürogebäude. Er dient als Empfangs- und Aufenthaltsbereich und weist eine extrem zarte Struktur auf. Der Innenhof ist als Garten gestaltet. Durch die völlig transparenten Fassaden wird der Bezug zum Garten hergestellt. Das Dach bildet eine Glasscheibe mit einem Durchmesser von 14 Meter. Das Glas ist weiß emailliert, die einzelnen Glasplatten sind an vier Punkten unterstützt. Die Scheibe wird von Stahlseilen getragen. Diese erreichen ihre Tragfähigkeit durch Verspannung an einem Stahlring. Der Stahlring liegt auf kreuzförmigen Stützen aus Edelstahl.

Die Struktur des Pavillons besteht aus einem doppelten elliptischen Ring aus Rohren, die sich im Randbereich befinden. Der Ring wird von vier kreuzförmigen Stützen getragen. Dieser Träger bildet einen Druckring, der zur Verspannung eines doppelten Seilnetzes dient. Die beiden Seilkonstruktionen sind mit Druckstäben aus Edelstahl verbunden. Durch die unterschiedliche Länge der Stäbe wird die parabolische Form des ersten Seilnetzes erreicht. Sie steifen das Glasdach aus und dienen der Abtragung der Lasten, die normal zur Glasebene wirken.

Roof construction detail

Exterior view

Interior room

1996–2000
Zurich Theater, Cultural Center and Workshop Zurich, Switzerland Ortner & Ortner

Ortner & Ortner won the competition to build the cultural center and workshops for the Zurich Theater consisting of workshops, rehearsal stages, an off-stage, apartments and an office building. They also built a restaurant, the Moods Jazz Club and a theater hall in the shipbuilding hall close by, which is a protected landmark.

The functional buildings were embellished with playful elements, such as the enlarged cement cast relief depicting the selection of Erechtheion.

Ortner & Ortner describe their building: *"The Zurich Festival House built its project on the former Sulzer-Escher-Wyss industrial estate in the western part of town. The building is a simple block that is 84 meters long, 40 meters wide and 23 meters high. All four sides feature vertical cement grooves with gold-framed ribbons of windows in between of matching width. On the inside, the building consolidates all the functions the theater requires. The workshops are located on the ground floor. These rooms occupy one and a half levels. On top of this section lie the offices and other required smaller rooms. A white ring of two and a half floor residential units with rooftop terraces facing both the courtyard and the city is located at the very top. Along its length, the building features a connecting wing which houses the rehearsal stages and he small theater hall, which is connected with the landmark shipbuilding hall."*

Ortner & Ortner gewannen 1996 den Wettbewerb für die Errichtung des Kultur- und Werkzentrums des Schauspielhauses Zürich, bestehend aus Werkstätten, Probebühnen, einer Off-Bühne, Wohnungen und einem Bürohaus. In der denkmalgeschützten ehemaligen Schiffbauhalle errichteten sie ein Restaurant, den Jazzclub Moods und das Hallentheater.

Die funktionalen Bauten sind mit spielerischen Elementen angereichert. Dazu zählen beispielsweise die vergrößerten Betonabgüsse der Reliefs der Koren des Erechtheion.

Ortner & Ortner beschreiben ihren Bau: *„Auf dem ehemaligen Industriegelände von Sulzer-Escher-Wyss im Westen der Stadt errichtet das Schauspielhaus Zürich seinen Hof. Der Hof zeigt sich als lapidarer Block 84 m lang, 40 m breit, 23 m hoch. Auf allen vier Seiten eine Fassade aus vertikalen Beton-Lisenen, dazwischen goldgefasste Fensterbänder in gleicher Breite. Im Inneren fasst der Hof die Nutzungen zusammen, die das Theater braucht. Ebenerdig über eineinhalb Geschosse die Werkstätten, darüber um einen bespielbaren Innenhof die Büros und was an kleineren Räumen gebraucht wird. Ganz oben ein weißer Ring von aneinandergereihten, zweieinhalbgeschoßigen schmalen Wohnhäusern mit Dachterrassen sowohl zum Hof als auch zur Stadt. An seiner Längsseite ist der Bau mit einem hohen Zwischentrakt, in dem sich drei Probebühnen und das kleine Theater befinden, an die denkmalgeschützte Schiffbauhalle angeschlossen."*

Overview of the entire project

Court Theater

Staircase

1996–2001
Austrian Embassy
Berlin, Germany
Hans Hollein

Hans Hollein won the two-stage, EU-wide competition (201participants) that was held in 1996/97 to build the Austrian Embassy in Berlin. The building at the beginning of the "Embassy Mile" serves as an embassy, consulate and residence. Its location on a corner is meant to emphasize its position as a link between the block construction on Stauffenbergstraße and the solitary character of the other side of the site.

In accordance with its three uses, the building is structured in three overlapping parts. One part is the four-level building block along Stauffenbergstraße that creates a U-shaped pattern together with the villa segment at the back of the site. The link side features an elliptically shaped, three-dimensional structure that is the site of the embassy's festive and representative functions.

A particularly representative sequence of rooms was given a privileged location. They are part of the sculpted entrance structure and extend over two floors on the upper level and include a gallery. This section's large panoramic windows face the zoo. The building has a main foyer that opens at the meeting point between the consular services block and the copper-clad ellipse. The foyer features an open, multi-level staircase that offers space for a reception line and for cultural events.

Hans Hollein ging als Sieger bei dem 1996/97 veranstalteten zweistufigen EU-weiten Architekturwettbewerb (201 Teilnehmer) für die österreichische Botschaft in Berlin hervor. Das Gebäude gegenüber dem Tiergarten am Beginn der „Botschaftsmeile" dient als Botschaft, Konsulat und Residenz. Die Eckbebauung versteht sich als Gelenk, das sowohl der Blockbebauung der Stauffenbergstraße verpflichtet ist, als auch dem Solitärcharakter, der die Bebauungsstruktur der anderen Seite des Grundstücks prägt.

Entsprechend der dreifachen Nutzung ist das Gebäude in drei Teile gegliedert, die ineinandergeschoben sind. Ein viergeschossiger entlang der Stauffenbergstraße gelegener Gebäuderiegel bildet gemeinsam mit dem im hinteren Grundstücksbereich liegenden Villengebäude eine U-Form. An der Gelenksstelle befindet sich ein ellipsoid geschwungener, plastischer Baukörper, der den Fest- und Repräsentationsteil der Botschaft aufnimmt.

Eine besonders repräsentative Raumfolge liegt an privilegierter Stelle. Als Teil des skulpturalen Eingangsbaukörpers erstreckt sie sich in den Obergeschossen über zwei Etagen mit umlaufender Galerie und orientiert sich mit großem Panoramafenster zum Tiergarten. Dort, wo der steinerne Konsulatsriegel und die kupferverkleidete Ellipse aufeinanderstoßen, öffnet sich ein etagenübergreifendes Hauptfoyer mit einer mehrgeschossigen Freitreppe, das Raum für den Empfang mit „reception-line" und für kulturelle Vorstellungen bietet.

Frontispiece, copper cladding

Stauffenbergstraße façade, office wing and frontispiece

Ambassador's residence

Main staircase

Ceremonial Hall

1997–2001
Munich Studio Theater, New Building
Munich, Germany
Gustav Peichl

The available space at the Munich Studio Theater had been insufficient for years. This affected rehearsals in particular. The new building alleviated this situation somewhat but also represented a challenge in terms of landmark preservation. Richard Riemerschmid built the old studio theater on Maximilianstraße in 1901. It is the one of the most important samples of Jugendstil architecture in Munich. The new building made it possible to keep this house in operation despite the changing demand for modern stage technology.

A competition was announced in 1990, after which Gustav Peichl's design was recommended for construction. Construction only began in 1997 in collaboration with Walter Achatz and Stefan Schumer due to financial difficulties.

The construction of the new Munich Studio Theater building was broken down into three segments: 1. The new rehearsal building, 2. The new workshop building and 3. The complete refurbishment of the main building. The rehearsal building was designed to be able to provide an alternate venue for performances while the refurbishment of the main building was underway. Parallel performances can be held on two of the three stages. The halls are stacked on top of each other, *"and create an impressive hollow core that is surrounded by all the required functions. A simplicity that lies between bleakness and asceticism dominates the interior. The halls and foyers are narrow, the steps are simple and the intermission rooms are stark. The only sumptuous element is the impressive technical equipment..."* (H. Wefing)

Das den Münchener Kammerspielen zur Verfügung stehende Raumangebot entsprach seit Jahren nicht den Erfordernissen. Besonders betroffen war davon der Probenbetrieb. Der Neubau schafft Abhilfe stellt aber auch ein Stück Denkmalspflege dar. Das alte Schauspielhaus in der Maximilianstraße, von Richard Riemerschmid 1901 erbaut, ist eines der bedeutendsten Beispiele der Jugendstilarchitektur Münchens. Mit dem Neuen Haus gelingt es dieses Haus trotz veränderter Ansprüche an eine zeitgemäße Bühnentechnik lebensfähig zu halten.

1990 wurde ein Wettbewerb ausgeschrieben, bei dem Gustav Peichls Entwurf zur Ausführung empfohlen wurde. Wegen finanzieller Probleme konnte erst 1997 in Zusammenarbeit mit Walter Achatz und Stefan Schumer mit dem Bau begonnen werden.

Der Neubau der Münchener Kammerspiele gliedert sich in drei Bauabschnitte: 1. Neubau des Probengebäudes, 2. Neubau des Werkstättengebäudes, 3. Generalsanierung des Haupthauses. Das Probengebäude wurde dabei von Anfang an so konzipiert, dass es während der Generalsanierung des Haupthauses die Spielstätten aufnehmen kann. Von den drei darin befindlichen Bühnen können zwei parallel bespielt werden. Die Säle sind übereinander gestapelt *„und bilden einen mächtigen hohlen Kern, der von allen dienenden Funktionen umstellt ist. Im Inneren regiert eine Schlichtheit, die zwischen Armut und Askese changiert. Die Flure und Foyers sind schmal, die Treppen einfach, die Pausenräume nachgerade karg. Üppig ist nur die famose technische Ausstattung. ..."* (H. Wefing)

Design sketch

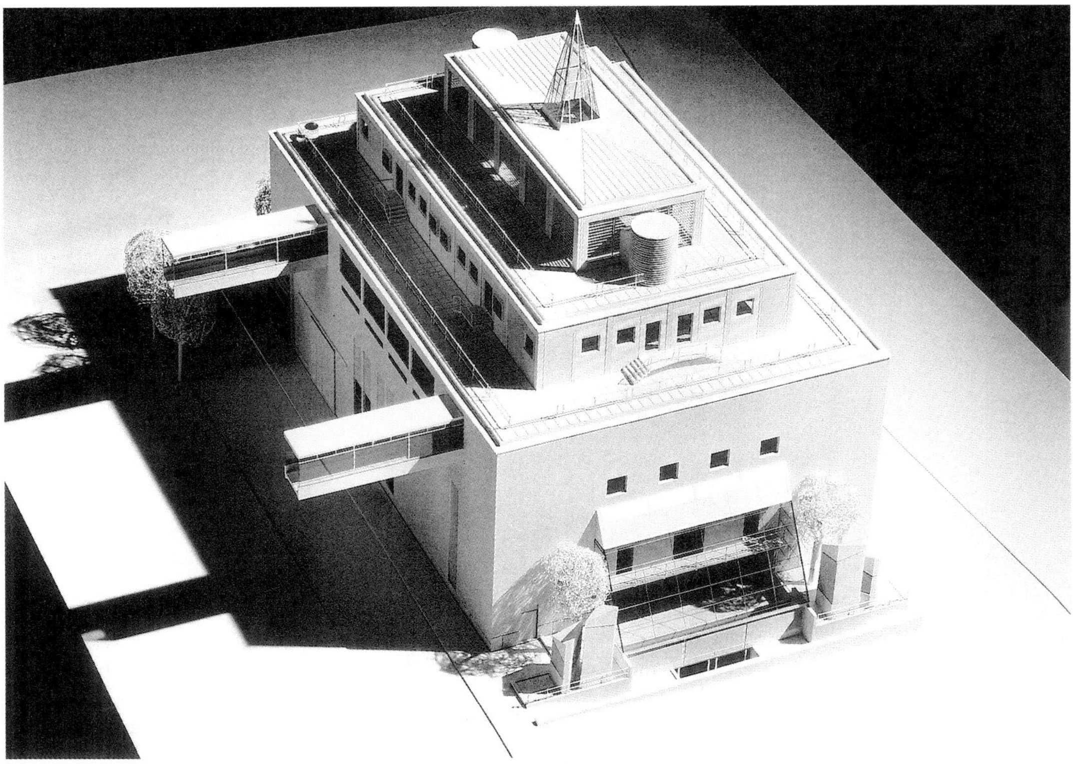

Model

Complete view from Neuturmstraße

Complete view from Hildegardstraße

View from the south of the roof with the light pyramid over the meeting room on the sixth floor

Foyer with visitor's gallery and Han Hoover sculpture

1997–2001
Haus am Gendarmenmarkt
Berlin, Germany
Heinz Tesar

A building was missing on the corner of Markgrafen-/Mohrenstraße on the Gendarmenmarkt Square in Berlin to complete construction on the site. Three architects shared the design of the surface, which contains five office, residential and commercial buildings that were designated the "Quartier 30": Claude Vasconi from Paris, Jo Coenen from Maastricht and Heinz Tesar from Vienna. Many discussions were necessary before the varying styles were blended satisfactorily.

The architects envisioned an open building, which is why the inner courtyard was not covered. It can be reached from many sides. The courtyard was the architects tribute to the Berlin tradition of open courtyards.

Heinz Tesar had a complicated task: he was in charge of building along the 70-meter back wall of the Federal Ministry of Justice. Hence it was only possible for light to stream in from the courtyard. In addition to this, it was only possible to build to a height of 22 meters in space along the firewall that was only six meters wide. Tesar solved the problem by creating an artistically designed access hall, which receives light from above. Elongated cement benches accentuate the depth of the hall. A baroque wave on the upper end of the firewall marks the transition to the vaulted roof. The round eyes in it create surprising light effects. On the side facing the street, Tesar chose to work with a fine relief created with natural stone slabs of differing thickness placed on top of the structure.

Zur Vollendung des Gendarmenmarktes fehlte bis 1999 noch die Verbauung des Grundstücks an der Ecke Markgrafen-/Mohrenstraße. Drei Architekten teilten sich die Gestaltung der Fläche mit fünf Büro-, Wohn- und Geschäftshäusern, die gemeinsam die Bezeichnung „Quartier 30" erhielten: Claude Vasconi aus Paris, Jo Coenen aus Maastricht und Heinz Tesar aus Wien. Bei der Vereinigung der unterschiedlichen Stile wurde anfangs viel gestritten.

Den Architekten schwebte ein offenes Gebäude vor, weshalb der Innenhof nicht überdacht wurde. Er ist von mehreren Seiten zugänglich. Mit dem Innenhof knüpfen die Architekten an die Berliner Tradition der durchgehbaren Höfe an.

Heinz Tesar hatte eine komplizierte Aufgabe: Er sollte an die 70 Meter breite Rückwand des Bundesjustizministeriums anbauen. Dadurch konnte nur vom Innenhof her Licht einfallen. Außerdem durfte aus Sicherheitsgründen an die Brandwand auf sechs Meter Breite nur bis zu 22 Meter hoch gebaut werden. Tesar löste das Problem, indem er entlang der Wand eine künstlerisch gestaltete Erschließungshalle errichtete, in die von oben Licht fällt. Lang gestreckte Betonbänke betonen die Tiefe der Halle. Am oberen Ende der Brandwand leitet eine barocke Welle auf das Tonnendach über, dessen runde Okuli für überraschende Lichtschöpfungen in der Halle sorgen. Die Straßenfront gestaltete Tesar, indem er ein feines Relief, gebildet durch unterschiedliche Plattenstärken aus Naturstein, auf den Baukörper legte.

Access hall with cement benches

Exterior view

Overview of the entire Quartier 30 project (Claude Vasconi/Paris, Jo Coenen/Maastricht, Heinz Tesar/Vienna)

Courtyard view

Access hall with deciduous trees and ocular-shaped openings in the ceiling

1998–2001
Reichsparteitagsgelände Documentation Center
Nuremberg, Germany
Günther Domenig

The conference hall on the edge of the former Reichsparteitag assembly grounds was built between 1935 and 1941 using cement, bricks and precisely cut granite stones on the façade. At the end of WWII, a 275-meter long, and up 265 meter wide horseshoe-shaped building remained; it was blocked off by two structures built across its width. The conference hall's significance isn't based on its architectural forms, the materials or its Classicism, which outshines its Roman precursors. Instead it is the political historical aspects that make it important.

The "Dokumentationszentrum Reichsparteitagsgelände" was incorporated in the northern head of the building as the result of a competition that was held in 1998. The guiding principle of Günther Domenig's proposal was to literally take an "incisive" approach to the building and integrate an "arrow-like" form of architecture in the structure. Domenig later confessed that: *"Chills ran down my spine when I saw the insanity of Hitler's intentions here. It affected me greatly and made me afraid. I became afraid of the axles and the many right angles."*

Domenig placed the entrance to the left of the colossal arch, where he cut a slit diagonal to the course of the wall in the massive façade. This entrance rises through the building in the manner of a slanted arrow. It creates an accessible caesura between the headpieces and offers a pulpit perspective of the incomplete arena in the inner courtyard.

Die Kongresshalle am ehemaligen Reichsparteitagsgelände in Nürnberg wurde von 1935 bis 1941 aus Beton, Ziegeln und präzise zugeschnittenen Granitquadern als Fassadenverkleidung errichtet. Nach Kriegsende blieb ein unvollendeter 275 Meter langer und bis zu 265 Meter breiter hufeisenförmiger Rundbau, der von zwei Querbauten abgeriegelt ist, zurück. Die Kongresshalle erhält ihre Bedeutung nicht aus den Architekturformen, dem Baumaterial und seinem Klassizismus, der römische Vorbilder an Größe übertrifft, sondern durch die politisch-historische Komponente.

In den nördlichen Kopfbau wurde das „Dokumentationszentrum Reichsparteitagsgelände" als Ergebnis eines Wettbewerbs von 1998 eingebaut. Dem siegreichen Entwurf Günther Domenigs liegt das Konzept zugrunde, sich wörtlich „einschneidend" mit dem Bau auseinander zu setzen und eine „pfeilartige" Architektur einzubauen. Domenig gestand später: *„Mir ist es eiskalt den Rücken hinunter gelaufen, als ich den Wahnsinn sah, den der Hitler da vorhatte. Ich war im höchsten Maße berührt und verängstigt. Ich bekam Angst vor den Achsen, vor den vielen rechten Winkeln."*

Domenig plazierte den Eingang links von dem kolossalen Rundbogen, wo er einen Schlitz schräg zur Wandflucht in die massive Fassade schnitt. Dieser Eingang steigt als schräger Pfeil durch das Gebäude an und schafft als begehbare Zäsur zwischen den Kopfbauten eine kanzelartige Vogelschau auf die unvollendete Arena des Innenhofes.

Entrance side

Courtyard "arrow"

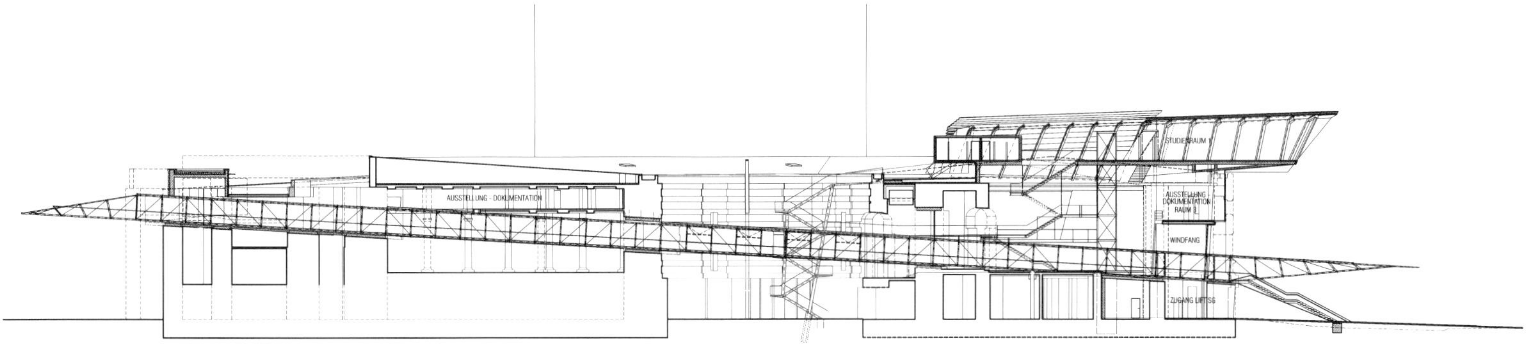

Section

Exhibition hall

Walkway "arrow"

Exhibition hall

1998–2002
Münchener Rück-Insurance Company Building
Munich, Germany
Baumschlager & Eberle

The "Münchener Rück" – an insurance company that insures insurance companies – expanded its headquarters in Schwabing, which was built in 1913, in two construction segments between 1969 and 1973. This was done with two buildings, one made of ferroconcrete and the other made of exposed aggregate concrete. Years later, the insurance company chose to atone for these architectural sins. The objective was to refurbish the existing building and optimize the office spaces (i.e.: improve workplace quality and eliminate the asbestos and insulation problems). Baumschlager & Eberle won the competition for this contract.

The idea the architects from Vorarlberg had was to build a fourth axle along the back of the three-axle structure with its dark middle zone and the offices built around it. This had a far-reaching effect on the building's configuration. The house is now aligned in a stringently horizontal manner and is a shimmering, glass-green structure now. The once 80 meter long block was remodeled as an s-shaped structure.

Major changes also took place on the inside: A 55 meter long and seven meter wide hall is connected to the glass canopy, its wall are clad with Canadian maple strips. The asymmetrically cut transoms in the roof allow for natural lighting. Walkways to the right and left lead to the two cores of the building and the elevators. The narrow office cells were consolidated as offices with two or more axles.

1969–73 erweiterte die „Münchener Rück" – eine Versicherung der Versicherungen – in zwei Bauetappen ihr 1913 errichtetes Stammhaus in Schwabing mit einem Bürohaus aus Stahlbeton und einer Waschbetonfassade. Die Versicherung entschloss sich dieses für seine Zeit typische Gebäude zu verändern. Es sollte das Haus unter Ausnutzung des bestehenden Bauwerks saniert und die Büroflächen optimiert (d. h.: die Qualität der Arbeitsplätze verbessert, die Asbest- und wärmetechnischen Probleme beseitigt) werden. Aus dem Wettbewerb dafür gingen Baumschlager & Eberle siegreich hervor.

Die Idee der Architekten war es, dem dreiachsigen Baukörper mit seiner dunklen Mittelzone und den rundumlaufenden Büros an der Rückseite eine vierte Achse anzubauen. Es entstand ein tiefer Einschnitt in die Gebäudekonfiguration. Das Haus ist nun sehr streng horizontal gegliedert und strahlt gläsern-grün. Der einstige 80 Meter lange Block wurde zu einem S-förmigen Gebilde umgestaltet.

Auch im Inneren fanden tiefgreifende Veränderungen statt: An den gläsernen Windfang schließt sich eine 55 Meter lange und sieben Meter breite Halle an, deren Wände mit kanadischen Ahornstäbchen verkleidet sind. Durch asymmetrisch in das Hallendach eingeschnittene Oberlichten wird der Raum natürlich belichtet. Nach links und rechts führen von hier Wege zu den beiden Kernen des Hauses mit den Liften. Die schmalen „Bürozellen" wurden zu zwei- oder mehrachsigen Büroräumen zusammengelegt.

Façade detail

Façade front

Entrance

Distribution room and lounge

Stairwell

future export

1998–
Passarelle Bercy-Tolbiac
Paris, France
Dietmar Feichtinger

View (Computer-generated photo collage)

View (Computer rendering)

2000–
Hamburg-Altona Train Station Center
Hamburg, Germany
Berger+Parkkinen

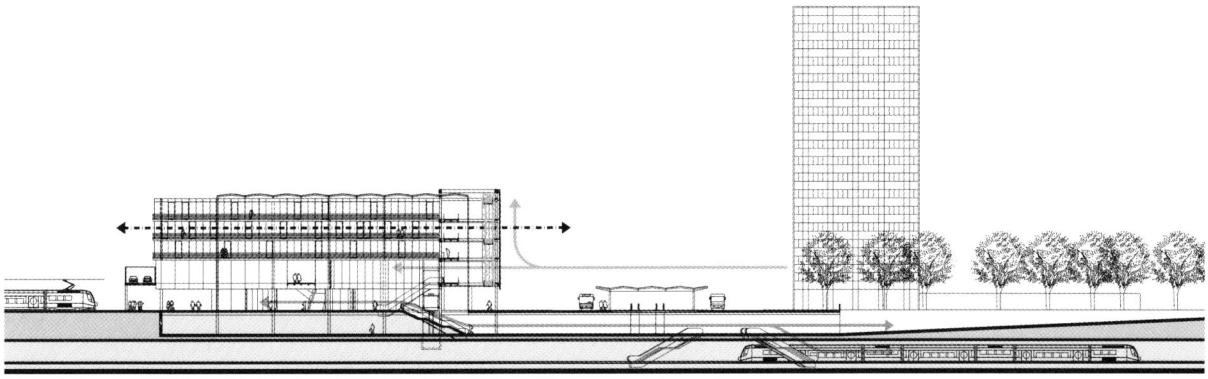

Section

Entrance (Computer rendering)

2000–
Quiagen Company
Biotechnical Production and Research Facility
Hilden/Düsseldorf, Germany
Szyszkowitz-Kowalski

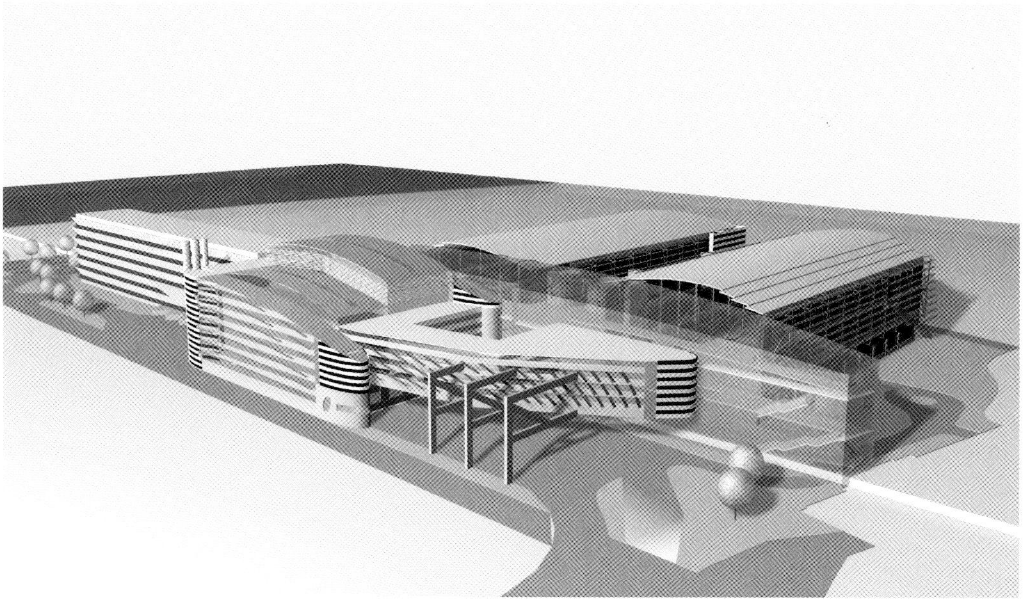

Overview (Computer rendering)

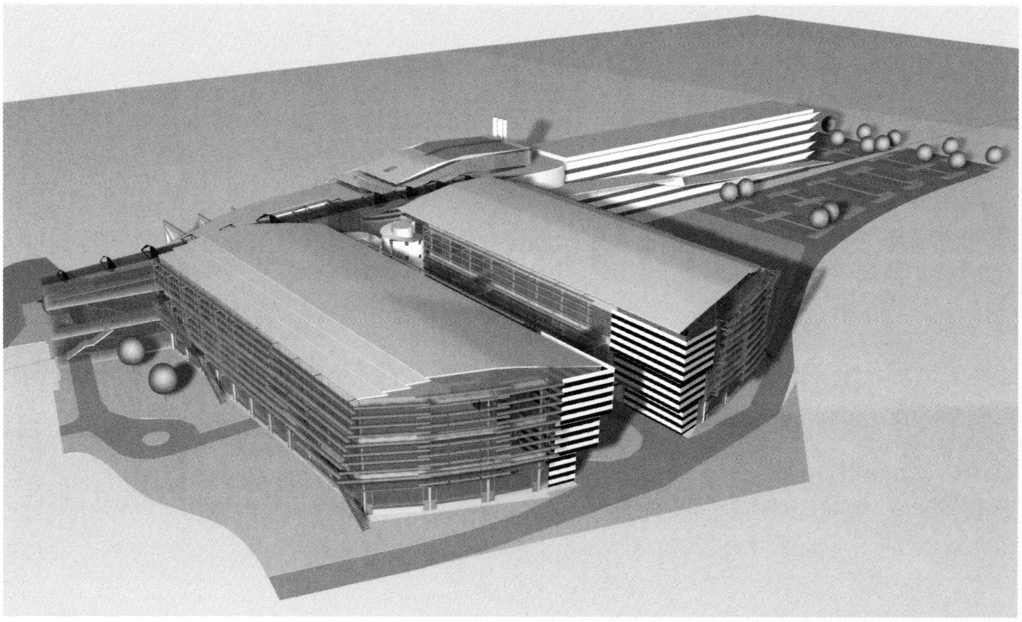

Overview (Computer rendering)

2001–
BMW Theme Park and Center
Munich, Germany
Coop Himmelb(l)au

Sketch

Exterior view

2001–
Bode Museum Refurbishment
Berlin, Germany
Heinz Tesar

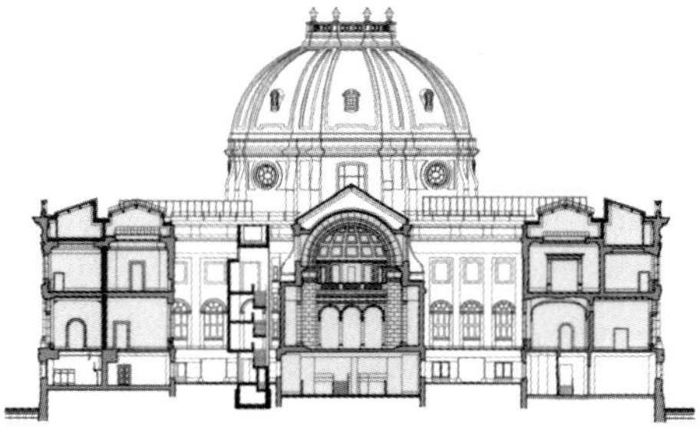

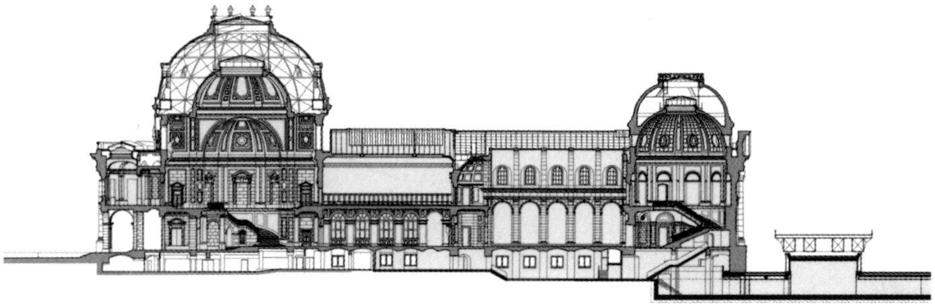

Longitudinal and cross section

Model section

2002–
Home for the Elderly "Wilhelm–Eck"
Berlin, Germany
Peichl + Partner

Façade Detail with a view of the uppermost level and corner solutions

Façade detail

2002–
ETH Zurich
Zurich, Switzerland
Baumschlager & Eberle

Overview (Computer rendering)

Corner view (Computer rendering)

2002–
ONUSIDA Geneva
Geneva, Switzerland
Baumschlager & Eberle

Section (Computer rendering)

Hall (Computer rendering)

2002–
Mont Saint Michel Walkway
Normandy, France
Dietmar Feichtinger

View (Computer generated photo collage)

2003–
Stadtpark Office Building
Nuremberg, Germany
Szyszkowitz-Kowalski

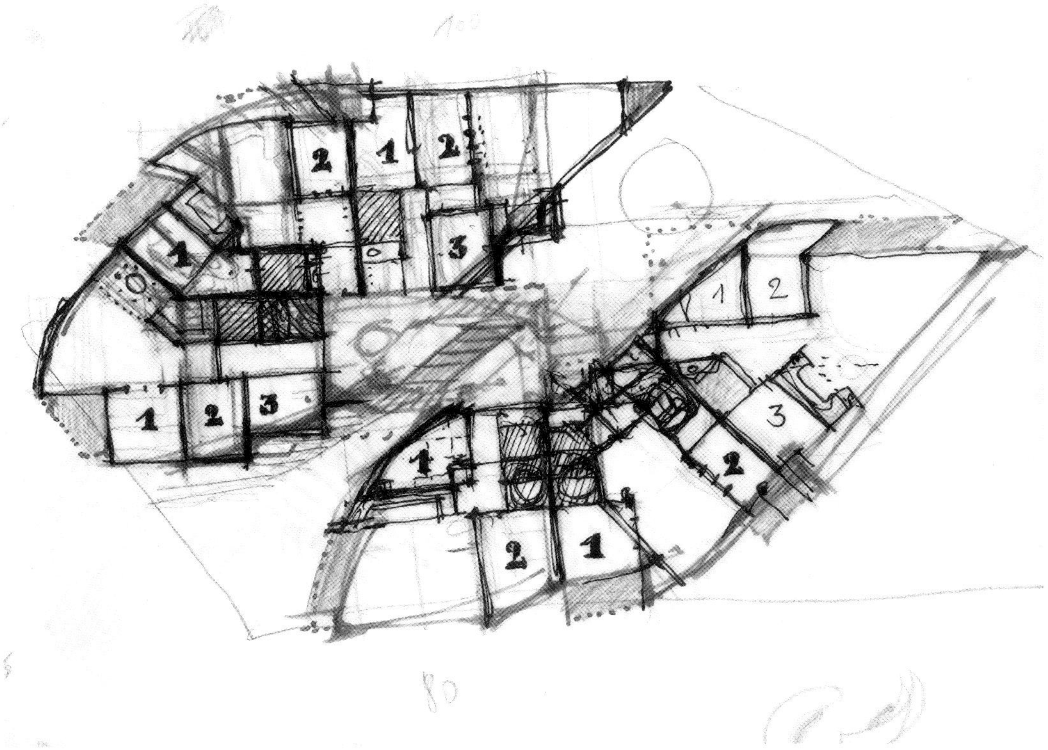

Floorplan sketch

Overview (Computer rendering)

2003–
Goetheplatz Square Design-Piazza d'Italia
Wolfsburg, Germany
Szyszkowitz-Kowalski

View (Computer rendering)

View by night (Computer rendering)

architects | architekten

Baumschlager & Eberle

CARLO BAUMSCHLAGER

Born in 1956 in Bregenz, Vorarlberg, he studied industrial design (under Hans Hollein) and Architecture (under Ungers and Wilhelm Holzbauer) at the Academy of Applied Arts in Vienna (graduated 1982).

wurde 1956 in Bregenz geboren und studierte Industrie-Design (bei Prof. Hollein), dann Architektur (bei Prof. Ungers und Prof. Holzbauer) an der Hochschule für angewandte Kunst in Wien (Diplom 1982).

DIETMAR EBERLE

Born in 1952 in Hittisau/Bregenzerwald, Vorarlberg, he studied at Vienna Technical University (under Professor Schweighofer, graduated 1978).

wurde 1952 in Hittisau/Bregenzerwald geboren und studierte an der Technischen Universität in Wien (Diplom 1978 bei Prof. Schweighofer).

The joint office was founded in 1985. Since then, they have completed numerous projects, among them: housing, schools, office and industrial buildings, as well as public buildings.

Das gemeinsame Büro wurde 1985 gegründet. Seither entstanden unzählige Projekte, darunter Wohnbauten, Schulen, Büro- und Industriebauten, öffentliche Gebäude.

Berger + Parkkinen

ALFRED BERGER

Born 1961 in Schwarzach/Salzburg, he studied architecture at Vienna Technical University from 1979 to 1983 before continuing his studies at the Academy of Fine Arts in Vienna (under Timo Penttilä) between 1983 and 1989. Partnership with Timo Penttilä and Werner Krismer that lasted from 1992 until 1994. He then taught at the Academy of Fine Arts in Vienna (Timo Penttilä, Massimiliano Fuksas) from 1994 until 1997 and also founded 1995 Berger + Parkkinen, Architects, Vienna-Helsinki in 1995.

geboren 1961 in Schwarzach/Salzburg, 1979-83 Architekturstudium an der TU Wien, 1983-89 Architekturstudium an der Akademie der bildenden Künste Wien (Prof. Timo Penttilä). 1992-94 Partnerschaft mit Timo Penttilä und Werner Krismer, 1994-97 Lehrtätigkeit an der Akademie der bildenden Künste in Wien (Prof. Timo Penttilä, Prof. Massimiliano Fuksas), 1995 Gründung des Büros Berger + Parkkinen Architekten, Wien-Helsinki.

TIINA PARKKINEN

Born 1965 in Vienna, Parkinnen studied architecture at the Academy of Fine Arts in Vienna (under Timo Penttilä) from 1984 until 1994, as well as urban planning in Fez, Morocco in 1986. She became a member of SAFA, the Chamber of Finnish Architects SAFA in 1994, and founded Berger + Parkkinen Architects, Vienna-Helsinki in 1995.

geboren 1965 in Wien, 1984-94 Architekturstudium an der Akademie der bildenden Künste Wien (Prof. Timo Penttilä), 1986 Städtebaustudien in Fes, Marokko, 1994 Eintritt in die Finnische Architektenkammer SAFA, 1995 Gründung des Büros Berger + Parkkinen Architekten, Wien-Helsinki.

Coop Himmelb(l)au

The COOP HIMMELB(L)AU **team was founded in 1968 in Vienna by Wolf D. Prix (born in 1942) and Helmut Swiczinsky (born in 1944). The team opened a second studio in 1988 in Los Angeles. The team received the Great Austrian State Award in 1999. Coop Himmelb(l)au has designed projects ranging from conversions to urban development projects in France. Coop Himmelb(l)au projects have been displayed at many exhibitions around the world.**

Das Team wurde 1968 von Wolf D. Prix (geboren 1942) und Helmut Swiczinsky (geboren 1944) in Wien gegründet. 1988 wurde ein zweites Atelier in Los Angeles eröffnet. 1999 erhielten Coop Himmelb(l)au den Großen Österreichischen Staatspreis. Coop Himmelb(l)au realisierte Projekte, die von Umbauten bis zu Stadtplanungsprojekten in Frankreich reichen. Die Arbeiten von Coop Himmelb(l)au wurden in vielen Ausstellungen auf der ganzen Welt gezeigt.

Günther Domenig

Born in 1934 in Klagenfurt/Carinthia, Domenig studied architecture at Graz Technical University (graduated 1959). He formed a partnership with Eilfried Huth that lasted from 1963 until 1973. He has maintained offices in Graz, Klagenfurt and Vienna since 1973 and acted as a partner on projects abroad as of 1987. He has been a visiting professor at a number of institutions both in Austria and abroad. He was named professor for housing development and design at the Institute for Construction Theory at Graz Technical University in 1980. Domenig is the founder and main proponent of the 'Graz School'.

geboren 1934 in Klagenfurt/Kärnten. Architekturstudium an der TU Graz (Diplom 1959). 1963-73 Partnerschaft mit Eilfried Huth. Seit 1973 Architekturbüros in Graz, Klagenfurt und Wien, ab 1987 Projektpartnerschaften im Ausland. Zahlreiche Gastprofessuren im In- und Ausland, seit 1980 Professor für Wohnbau und Entwerfen am Institut für Gebäudelehre der TU Graz. Gründer und Hauptvertreter der "Grazer Schule".

Dietmar Feichtinger

Born in 1961 in Bruck an der Mur, Feichtinger studied architecture at Graz Technical University from 1981 to 1988 and received his diploma with an honorary mention. In 1989–93, he was associate architect and project manager at the offices of Philippe Chaix/Jean–Paul Morel in France. He has worked independently in Paris since 1994. Feichtinger also taught at the UP 6 - La Villette University in Paris from 1994–9 and has cooperated closely with Peter Rice et Associés (RFR) since. In 1995, he was also a visiting professor at Innsbruck University from 1994 until 1997, before being appointed to teach at Vienna Technical University.

geboren 1961 in Bruck an der Mur. 1981–88 Architekturstudium an der Technischen Universität Graz, Diplom mit Auszeichnung. 1989–93 Assoziierter Architekt und Projektleiter im Büro Philippe Chaix/Jean-Paul Morel Frankreich. Seit 1994 selbständige Tätigkeit mit Bürositz in Paris. 1994–99 Lehrauftrag an der Pariser Universität UP 6-La Villette. Seit 1995 enge Zusammenarbeit mit Peter Rice et Associés (RFR). 1995 Gastprofessur an der Universität Innsbruck, 1994–97 Lehrauftrag an der Universität Innsbruck, 1997 Lehrauftrag an der Technischen Universität Wien.

Hans Hollein

Born in Vienna in 1934, Hollein studied architecture under Clemens Holzmeister from 1953 until 1956 at the Academy of Fine Arts in Vienna. He worked in Stockholm as an architect, urban planner and designer between 1956 and 1958 before continuing his studies in the USA at the Illinois Institute of Technology and at the University of California, Berkeley. He was a visiting professor at Washington University St. Louis/Missouri from 1963 to 1964 and again in 1966. Hollein established his own office in Vienna in 1964 before becoming a professor at the State Academy of Art in Düsseldorf from 1967 until 1976. He was then appointed professor at the University of Applied Arts in Vienna where he taught from 1976 until 2002. He was awarded the Great Austrian State Prize in 1983 and won the Pritzker Prize in 1985.

geboren 1934 in Wien. 1953–56 Studium an der Akademie der bildenden Künste in Wien bei Clemens Holzmeister, 1956–58 als Architekt, Städteplaner und Designer in Stockholm, 1958–60 weitere Studien in den USA am Illinois Institute of Technology und an der University of California, Berkeley, 1963–64 und 1966 Gastprofessor an der Washington University St. Louis/Missouri, seit 1964 eigenes Büro in Wien, 1967–76 Professor an der Staatlichen Kunstakademie in Düsseldorf, 1976–2002 Professor an der Hochschule (Universität) für angewandte Kunst in Wien, 1983 Großer Österreichischer Staatspreis, 1985 Pritzker-Preis.

Wilhelm Holzbauer

Born in 1930 in Salzburg, Holzbauer studied at the Salzburg State Trade School from 1945 until 1949 before attending the Vienna Academy of Fine Arts and training under Clemens Holzmeister from 1950 until 1953. He then attended M.I.T in Cambridge/USA from 1956 until 1957. Holzbauer collaborated with Friedrich Kurrent and Johannes Spalt in Arbeitsgruppe 4 (Work Group 4) and was a visiting professor at Yale University in New Haven/USA between 1958 and 1959. He opened his own office in Vienna in 1964 and another office in Amsterdam in 1969. He won the 1972 Architecture Award of the City of Vienna in 1972, before becoming a visiting professor at Graz Technical University from 1974 to 1976. Holzbauer later was appointed professor at the University of Applied Arts, where he taught from 1977 until 1998. He was awarded the Great Austrian State Prize in 2000.

geboren 1930 in Salzburg. 1945–49 Studium an der Staatsgewerbeschule in Salzburg, 1950–53 an der Wiener Akademie der bildenden Künste bei Clemens Holzmeister, 1956–57 am M.I.T. in Cambridge/USA, 1952–64 Zusammenarbeit mit Friedrich Kurrent und Johannes Spalt im Rahmen der Arbeitsgruppe 4, 1958–59 Gastprofessor an der Yale University, New Haven/USA, seit 1964 eigenes Büro in Wien und seit 1969 in Amsterdam, 1972 Architekturpreis der Stadt Wien, 1974–76 Gastprofessor an der Technischen Hochschule in Graz, 1977–98 Professor an der Hochschule für angewandte Kunst in Wien, 2000 Großer Österreichischer Staatspreis.

Szyszkowitz-Kowalski

MICHAEL SZYSZKOWITZ

Born in 1944 in Graz, Michael Szyszkowitz studied architecture at Graz Technical University. He opened a joint office with Karla Kowalski in 1973 and has been a professor at Braunschweig Technical University since 1988.

geboren 1944 in Graz. Architekturstudium an der TU Graz. Seit 1973 Architekturbüro mit Karla Kowalski in Frankfurt, München und vor allem in Graz. Seit 1988 Professor an der TU Braunschweig.

KARLA KOWALSKI

Born 1941 in Upper Silesia, Karla Kowalski studied architecture at Darmstadt Technical University from 1962 until 1968 before beginning her postgraduate studies in London (1968–69). She opened a joint office with Michael Szyszkowitz 1973 and has been a professor at Stuttgart Technical University since 1988.

geboren 1941 in Oberschlesien. 1962–68 Architekturstudium an der TU Darmstadt, Postgraduate Studium in London (1968–69). Seit 1973 Architekturbüro mit Michael Szyszkowitz. Seit 1988 Professorin an der TU Stuttgart.

Ortner & Ortner

LAURIDS ORTNER

Born in 1941 in Linz, Laurids Ortner studied architecture at Vienna Technical University between 1959 and 1965. Co-founder of the Haus-Rucker-Co group of architects and artists in Vienna. He opened the Haus-Rucker-Co group studio in Düsseldorf (1970–87) along with Günter Zamp Kelp and Manfred Ortner. Laurids Ortner has been a professor of architecture at the State Art Academy in Düsseldorf since 1987.

geboren 1941 in Linz. 1959–65 Architekturstudium an der TU Wien. Mitbegründer der Architekten- und Künstlergruppe Haus-Rucker-Co in Wien. 1970–87 Atelier Haus-Rucker-Co in Düsseldorf mit Günter Zamp Kelp und Manfred Ortner. Seit 1987 Professor für Baukunst an der Staatlichen Kunstakademie in Düsseldorf.

MANFRED ORTNER

Born in 1943 in Linz, Manfred Ortner studied painting and the fine arts at the Academy of Fine Arts and history at the University of Vienna between 1961 and 1967. He was also a co-founder of the Haus-Rucker-Co studio in Düsseldorf (1971–87) along with Günter Zamp Kelp and Laurids Ortner. Ortner has been a professor for design at the Potsdam Specialized College since 1994.

geboren 1943 in Linz. 1961–67 Studium der Malerei und Kunsterziehung an der Akademie der bildenden Künste und Studium der Geschichte an der Universität in Wien. 1971–87 Atelier Haus-Rucker-Co mit Günter Zamp Kelp und Laurids Ortner. Seit 1994 Professor für Entwerfen an der Architekturfakultät der FH Potsdam.

The brothers founded the Ortner & Ortner Studio in Vienna in 1990, before opening their offices in Berlin in 1994.

1990 gründeten sie das Büro Ortner & Ortner in Wien, 1994 das Büro Ortner & Ortner in Berlin.

Gustav Peichl

Born in 1928 in Vienna, Peichl studied under Clemens Holzmeister at the Academy of Fine Arts from 1949 until 1953. In 1953, he attended the Salzburg Summer Academy and trained under Prof. Hofmann (Zurich). He has also worked as a political caricaturist since 1955 under the pen name of "Ironimus". He opened his own office in Vienna in 1956 and was the co-founder of "Bau" magazine in 1965. Peichl won the Great Austrian State Award in 1971 and was a professor as the Academy of Fine Arts in Vienna from 1973 to 1996. Participant at the Documenta in Kassel, the Biennale in Venice and the Triennale in Milan. Visiting professor in Harvard. Honorary member at the Royal Institute of British Architects and the American Institute of Architects.

geboren 1928 in Wien. Studium an der Akademie der bildenden Künste bei Clemens Holzmeister (1949–53). 1953 Teilnahme an der Salzburger Sommerakademie bei Prof. Hofmann (Zürich), seit 1955 als politischer Karikaturist unter dem Pseudonym „Ironimus" tätig, seit 1956 eigenes Architekturbüro in Wien, 1965 Mitbegründer der Zeitschrift „Bau", 1971 Großer Österreichischer Staatspreis, 1973–1996 Professor an der Akademie der bildenden Künste in Wien. Teilnehmer der Documenta in Kassel, der Biennale in Venedig und der Triennale in Mailand. Gastprofessor in Harvard. Ehrenmitglied des Royal Institute of British Architects und des American Institute of Architects.

Heinz Tesar

Born in 1939 in Innsbruck, Tesar studied architecture at the Academy of Fine Arts in Vienna (under Roland Rainer). He has taught at various universities in Europe and the United States since the 1980s and has an office in Vienna and Berlin with ten staff members. He was awarded the Gold Heinrich-Tessenow medal in 2000.

geboren 1939 in Innsbruck, Studium der Architektur an der Akademie der bildenden Künste (Meisterklasse Roland Rainer) in Wien. Seit den 1980er Jahren lehrt Tesar an verschiedenen Universitäten in Europa sowie Amerika und hat Ateliers in Wien und Berlin, wo zehn Mitarbeiter tätig sind. 2000 wurde Heinz Tesar mit der Heinrich-Tessenow-Medaille in Gold geehrt.

Ottokar Uhl

Born in 1931 in Wolfsberg/Carinthia, Uhl attended the Academy of Fine Arts in Vienna from 1950 until 1953 (Lois Welzenbacher Master Class). He was appointed professor for church construction at the Academy of Fine Arts in Vienna in 1965 and taught there until 1972. He was also a visiting professor (industrial construction) at Washington University in the USA from 1969 until 1970, before accepting an appointment to teach at the Academy of Fine Arts in Vienna (Architecture and Art Appreciation). He was made a full professor at Karlsruhe University, where he taught from 1973 until 1994 (Construction Planning Chair). Uhl has published a number of articles and research papers.

geboren 1931 in Wolfsberg/Kärnten, 1950–53 Besuch der Akademie der bildenden Künste in Wien (Meisterklasse Lois Welzenbacher). 1965–72 Lehrauftrag an der Akademie der bildenden Künste in Wien (Kirchenbau), 1969–70 Gastprofessor an der Washington University in den USA (industrialisiertes Bauen), 1971–75 Lehrauftrag an der Akademie der bildenden Künste in Wien (Architektur und Kunsterziehung), 1973–94 ordentlicher Univ.-Prof. an die Universität Karlsruhe/Germany (Lehrstuhl für Bauplanung). Veröffentlichungen zahlreicher Forschungsarbeiten.

Credits

2. Gustav Peichl, Wien
12. Archiv Markus Kristan, Wien
13. Archiv Markus Kristan, Wien
14. Archiv Markus Kristan, Wien
15. l: Josef M. Olbrich, 1867-1908, Katalog, Darmstadt 1983
15. r: Archiv Markus Kristan, Wien
16. l: Eduard F. Sekler: Josef Hoffmann, Salzburg - Wien 1982
16. r: Archiv Markus Kristan, Wien
17. Albertina, Wien; © VBK Wien, 2003
18. Stadtmuseum Nordico, Linz
19. Archiv Markus Kristan, Wien
20. l: Akademie der bildenden Künste (Hrsg.): Clemens Holzmeister, Katalog, Wien 1982
20. r: Archiv Markus Kristan, Wien
21. r: August Sarnitz: Lois Welzenbacher, Wien 1989
22. Lisa Philips: Frederick Kiesler, New York 1989
23–25l: Archiv Markus Kristan, Wien
25. r: Peter Noever, MAK (Hrsg.): Margarete Schütte-Lihotzky, Wien 1993
26. l: Archiv Markus Kristan, Wien
26. r: Universität für angewandte Kunst (Hrsg.): Oswald Haerdtl, Wien 1978
27. Archiv Roland Rainer, Wien
28. l: August Sarnitz (Hrsg.): Bauen in Europa, Katalog, Wien - New York 1998
28. r: Archiv Günther Domenig, Graz
29. l: Marlies Darsow
29. r: August Sarnitz (Hrsg.): Bauen in Europa, Katalog, Wien - New York 1998
29. b: Gustav Peichl, Wien
33–37. Wilhelm Holzbauer, Wien
Fotos: Martha Popp-Deltsios, Wien
39–43. Atelier Klaus Kinold, München
45–49. Petra Wittmar & Ulrich Deimel, Essen
51–54. Gustav Peichl, Wien
Fotos: Peter Oszvald, Bonn
55. Gustav Peichl, Wien
Foto: Monika Nikolic, Kassel
57. Wilhelm Holzbauer, Wien
Foto: Stefan Olah, Wien
58–59. Wilhelm Holzbauer, Wien
Fotos: Martha Popp-Deltsios, Wien
61–65. Stefan Müller, Berlin
67–69. Szyszkowitz-Kowalski, Graz
Fotos: Karla Kowalski, Graz
71–75. Margherita Spiluttini, Wien
77. Punctum & Schink, Leipzig
78–81. Gerald Zugmann, Wien
83–87. Christian Richters, Münster
89–91. Eduard Hueber, New York
93. Martin Frank
94. Gert von Bassewitz, Hamburg
95. Michael Scholz, Berlin
96–97. Paul Ott, Graz
99–103. Vulcania-Joël Damase, Clermont-Ferrand
105–107, 109. Wilhelm Holzbauer, Wien
Foto: Rupert Steiner, Wien
108. Wilhelm Holzbauer, Wien
Foto: Kohl & Olah, Wien
111–115. Stefan Müller, Berlin
117–121. Berger + Parkkinen, Wien
Fotos: Christian Richters, Münster
123–125. Dietmar Feichtinger, Paris
127–129. Margherita Spiluttini, Wien
131–135. Florian Bolk, Berlin
137. Gustav Peichl, Wien
138–141. Gustav Peichl, Wien
Fotos: Gisela Erlacher, Wien
143–147. Christian Richters, Münster
149–153. Gerald Zugmann, Wien
155–159. Eduard Hueber, New York
162. Dietmar Feichtinger, Paris
163. Berger + Parkkinen, Wien
164. Szyszkowitz-Kowalski, Graz
165. Coop Himmelb(l)au, Wien
166. Heinz Tesar, Wien
167. Gustav Peichl, Wien
Fotos: Heinrich Hermes, Berlin
168. Baumschlager & Eberle, Lochau
169. Baumschlager & Eberle, Lochau